F ROWS OF BARBED WIRE

The Immigrants Journey
The Truth Told Nearly a Century Later

The True Oskar Bendl Story

Inspired by the book
Both Sides of the Wire
by Ted Jones

and

Our grandparents' journey to Canada
A Journey to Living Hell on Earth

JACK M. FRÉCHETTE

Five Rows of Barbed Wire
Copyright © 2018 by Jack M. Fréchette

All rights reserved. No part of this publication may be reproduced, distributed, or transmitted in any form or by any means, including photocopying, recording, or other electronic or mechanical methods, without the prior written permission of the author, except in the case of brief quotations embodied in critical reviews and certain other non-commercial uses permitted by copyright law.

Tellwell Talent
www.tellwell.ca

ISBN
978-0-2288-0453-6 (Hardcover)
978-0-2288-0452-9 (Paperback)

This book is dedicated in loving memory
of my mother, Joyce Fréchette (nee Bendl).

My Grandparents
Oskar and Theresia Bendl and Family
and all the POWs and their families
that suffered through a very
DARK CHAPTER IN CANADA'S HISTORY

FIVE ROWS OF BARBED WIRE

The Immigrants Journey

For family and reader,

Canada has always portrayed itself as a clean, picturesque, friendly country filled with many different nationalities, cultures, and traditions.

By world standards, Canada has been known as a country that respects and protects its citizens' human rights. That has not always been true, however.

Canada has a dark past, with many dark chapters that most Canadians are not aware of.

Canada's government, it would appear, prefers not to acknowledge its past history, preferring to keep those years hidden from scrutiny.

This book is about our grandparents, Oskar and Theresia Bendl, who immigrated to Canada from Austria in 1925, and the many other immigrants to Canada at that time.

In the late 1800s and early 1900s, tens of thousands of Europeans from across the war-torn continent journeyed to Canada and the United States. They were seeking a better life. They were brave people, and most would never see their homelands or families again.

If you stop and think about your family's history for just a moment, you'll see that we've all been immigrants to Canada at some point.

European history has always been a tangled web throughout the ages. It is important to know why those immigrants came to Canada, and what became of them. Their story began over one hundred years ago in Europe...

When I was young, my mother did not talk about our grandparents' immigration to Canada, or her family's early life. The only thing she said was, "We were as poor as church mice." It was a dark family secret, and it was only talked about in hushed tones among the adults, and those that were close friends of the family.

For many of us when we are young, our grandparents are mysterious people. We learn that they are our mothers' or fathers' parents, and then, they usually die before we learn much more.

As I got older, I learned that our grandfather had been a Prisoner of War in Canada during World War II, and later that we are the descendants of Austrian royalty.

I was fortunate, and old enough to have known our grandfather and grandmother. I was almost sixteen years of age when our grandfather passed away.

A few years later I spoke to our grandmother, Theresia, about their lives in Austria, and later (in 1995 and 1998) to her oldest son, Lou. He related much more of the family's history to me.

FIVE ROWS OF BARBED WIRE

When the Canadian government arrested our grandfather and seized his land in 1940, it was a horror that haunted all members of the Bendl family for decades. And more pain followed.

During World War II, tens of thousands of men were rounded up and imprisoned in Canada. Their wives and children were left behind and had to fend for themselves. In most cases the husband had been the "breadwinner" in those households. The burden of responsibility then fell on the wives of those that had been interned. What those women and children endured while the husband was imprisoned is beyond belief.

Our grandparents, however, probably lost more than most of the internees and their families.

Oskar Bendl has been written about in several books on internment in Canada, and many illustrations of his beautiful oil paintings have appeared as well. The books, however, do not tell you anything of his life or that of his family while he was imprisoned.

This book is a personal account of our grandparents, Oskar and Theresia Bendl's lives, and the other immigrants, that journeyed to Canada at that time. The immigrants were seeking a better life, and many were met with something that they were not expecting. I have woven their life stories through the 19th century, as history unfolded in their lives, to give you a better perspective and understanding of the immigrant's journey.

I had reservations about writing this book, as I have known many details of our grandparents' lives for many decades. Our grandparents' story is a disturbing one, and like them, I chose not to speak of the details, considering it "a black mark" on the family. The details are emotionally draining.

Many of you never knew your grandfather and were too young to really remember your grandmother. They were fine people. The story of their lives in Canada is a horrible story.

I have been encouraged by friends that read my earlier manuscripts to tell this story, as they felt "it was a story, that had to be told." I reconsidered because you have the right to know the details of your own grandparents' lives. As harsh as their lives were. Not wanting to allow the dust of time to bury the cruel history of their lives forever, I felt it would have been a tragedy not to have told you their story.

CHAPTERS

1. Centuries of War 1
2. Journey to Canada 39
3. Canada's Prisoner of War Camps and Other Camps 75
4. Oskar Bendl's Release and a Long Walk Home 119
5. Canada After World War II 125
6. Oskar and Theresia Bendl's Legacy 171
7. Summary 173
About this Book 181
Credits and Acknowledgements 185
Further Acknowledgements, and Thank Yous 187
About the Author 188

1.
CENTURIES OF WAR

Since the beginning of time, Man has fought with his neighbours. Governments have often felt threatened by countries that threaten countries that are allied to their own, and it has often resulted in war. Hundreds of millions of civilian lives have been taken throughout the ages by wars that were caused by governments. Sadly, many of those that died or suffered were people that had no choice or say in the matter. It is a very sad fact, that history has not taught mankind much throughout the ages.

Up until the 19th century, Europe had suffered thousands of years of wars. Wars have been evidenced as early as before 500 BC. Each decade from the 1st century through the 19th brought more and more wars, and civil unrest, throughout Europe.

The Napoleonic Wars of 1803–1815 were a series of major conflicts across Europe that put the French

Empire against a fluctuating array of European powers formed into various coalitions. The coalitions were usually financed and led by Great Britain.

Historians have categorized the five conflicts after the coalition that fought Napoleon. The Third Coalition 1805, The Fourth Coalition 1806–07, The Fifth Coalition 1809, The Sixth Coalition 1813, and The Seventh Coalition 1815.

In 1799, Napoleon seized power and ascended to First Consul of France, inheriting a chaotic republic. He set about creating a stable state with strong government and strong finances, and he built a very large, well-trained army.

Napoleon Bonaparte was born August 15, 1769 in Corsica, and was educated at a military school. He is considered one of history's greatest military leaders.

Napoleon's tactics on the battlefield were clever, and he remains famous for his victories. One of Napoleon's greatest tactics was to send a portion of his troops onto the battlefield and let the firing begin. After the enemy committed themselves he sent his armies around the enemy from behind and on both sides, then fight them in smaller groups, taking them by total surprise.

In 1800, Napoleon and his army defeated the Austrians at Marengo. May 18, 1803 is considered by many historians as the beginning of the Napoleonic wars. Britain ended The Treaty of Amiens and declared war on France in May 1803.

Russia felt that Napoleon's invasion of Switzerland had indicated that the French were not looking for peaceful solutions with the other European powers.

In 1805, Austria and Russia declared war on France. Napoleon responded and defeated the allied Russian-Austrian armies at Austerlitz in 1805, the War of the Third Coalition. Austerlitz is considered Napoleon's greatest victory. In the same year, the British inflicted a severe defeat upon a joint Franco-Spanish navy giving them control of the seas and preventing an invasion of Britain itself. Months later, Prussia declared war, triggering the War of the Fourth Coalition in 1806. Prussia was defeated in nineteen days. Napoleon then turned on Russia and defeated them at Friedland ending the Fourth Coalition in 1807.

Europe was in an uneasy state of peace. It did not last long, as war broke out two years later in 1809, and another coalition was quickly defeated.

Russia had been barred from trading with certain countries and was unwilling to bear the economic consequences. They violated the Continental System of Trade imposed on them, ending with dissolution, and withdrawal of the French Forces.

In 1809, the Austrian repulse of Napoleon at Aspern-Essling brought about a stalemate. It was not a victory, but it had shown Austria's allies that Napoleon could be defeated. Short lived, the Austrians lost at Wagram.

Angered by Russia's violation of the Continental System of Trade, Napoleon invaded Russia in 1812. Napoleon's campaign was a disaster. Desertions and the onset of a Russian winter stopped the invasion. Napoleon retreated having lost the bulk of his half-million soldier army.

The tide had begun to turn in favour of the Allies. France's military and financial losses were beginning to mount up.

An unlikely alliance took place as Austria, Prussia, Russia, and Great Britain—countries that were usually suspicious of their neighbours—came together. Encouraged by this, Austria, Prussia, and Russia began a new campaign against France.

In the early days of October 1813, an Austrian militia led by von Kamper met Napoleon's army on a battlefield in Saxony, near Leipzig, Germany.

von Kamper was a brilliant strategist and a great military leader. He had fought Napoleon, in previous battles. Outnumbered, von Kamper lost the battle, but re-grouped his troops later in the day. Napoleon was going somewhere else, to something much bigger, and von Kamper's army followed him.

A couple days later at Leipzig, von Kamper's militia and other Austrian militias, as well as Prussian, Russian, Swedish, and other armies met Napoleon's army on the battlefield.

von Kamper was our grandfather's, great-great grandfather. Naturally, we are all descendants of von Kamper as well. von Kamper was bestowed the royal title of "von" by the emperor for services to Austria. The Austrians had colonized Poland, and von Kamper's colony had been Krakow.

Our Uncle Lou told me that years later, von Kamper's daughter became so poor that she sold her title of "von," ending her once proud royal heritage. I have never been able to verify this information, however.

von Kamper's daughter

The Battle of Leipzig was, in terms of numbers of troops and amount of artillery, the biggest battle of the Napoleonic Wars and the largest battle on European soil before World War I. The battle has been referred to as The Battle of Nations.

Napoleon brought 300,000 men to Germany. He positioned corps in defensive locations in Hamburg and elsewhere to threaten the Prussian rear, as well as in nearby Dresden.

Separate but coordinated armies of Austrians, Prussians, Russians, Swedes, and others, brought 370,000 troops and almost 1,500 guns to the battlefield, whereas Napoleon's strength stood at 198,000 men with 717 guns. Austria's military had Europe's largest number of military horsemen, consisting of some 40,000. Many of those militia horsemen and 160,000 Austrians and Russians came to Leipzig for this battle.

The Leipzig battlefield was misty on the morning of, October 15, 1813. Napoleon had thwarted an early attack by Prince Karl von Schwarzenberg, field commander from Austria.

The Allies decided to attack Napoleon's smaller support armies, but avoid a major battle, a similar tactic that Napoleon had used in many battles.

The battle began when Napoleon seized the Leipzig position, intending to divide the enemy armies and attack them one by one. The French almost had that chance the very first day when the Prussian army engaged, while the Army of the North—a Russo-Prusso-Swedish force under Bernadotte, a former French Marshall—held back. Napoleon became the victim of his own repeated changes of operational focus that day.

Allied strength kept building the second day at Leipzig, as more troops arrived. Napoleon spent most of the day redeploying. He had to face Blücher's advancing armies from the north, and soon had to do an about-face to deal with the even larger Austrian Army of Bohemia approaching from the south. The Army of Bohemia numbered 160,000 Austrian and Russians commanded by Prince Karl von Schwarzenberg, of Austria, who was also the coalition's field commander at Leipzig.

Austrian Prince Karl von Schwarzenberg, Field Commander

Most of the damage on the battlefield at Leipzig was caused by the amount of artillery in use. As well as the guns, there were rifles, muskets, bayonets, pistols, spears, and swords used in close combat. At that time, the musket was not really an accurate weapon at three hundred feet. However, given the proximity to the enemy, when the musket was fired, it often did not hit the soldier that it had been shot at. It would often hit the soldier next to the soldier it had been fired at. The consequences most often, were deadly.

On the final day, the allied numbers and combat power became too much for the French, as their armies were surrounded by the Allies.

On October 18, Napoleon prepared for a withdrawal. That night he ordered his troops to retreat but ordered 30,000 troops to remain. In withdrawal there was disaster for the French. A premature destruction of a major river bridge at Leipzig trapped 30,000 French and killed over 2,000 on or near the bridge. Casualties for the battlefield have been estimated at 73,000 French and 55,000 Allies.

When the Battle of Leipzig ended, the battlefield was five square miles of blood-soaked earth. [a01]

Napoleon and his army of 100,000 retreated toward France. By the time the army reached Paris, desertion had reduced his army to about 60,000. Napoleon still held the throne of France, though it was only a matter of time before he would have to step down. He knew that his foes were coming for him, and he no longer had his half-million man army.

On November 8, 1813, the Allies offered France a peace settlement that would return France to borders behind the Alps, well back from the Rhine. Napoleon foolishly rejected that offer, and on December 21 the Allied armies crossed the Rhine and invaded France. During the first months of 1814, a few battles were fought across northern France, and the battle for Paris commenced on March 30. Napoleon abdicated unconditionally on April 11 and was exiled to the small island of Elba, off the coast of Italy.

On Elba, Napoleon lived like a king and was called the Emperor of Elba by the island's people. Napoleon's mother and sister both came to live with him there in separate mansions. Napoleon's wife was not allowed on the island, but Napoleon enjoyed the company of one of the island's girls, and his Polish mistress. Napoleon's exile would only last about three hundred days.

In March of 1815, he escaped and returned to Paris where he regained supporters. He reclaimed his emperor title, Napoleon I, in the period known as The Hundred Days. In June of that year he was defeated by the British at Waterloo in Belgium. The battle was a short but very bloody battle that ended Napoleon's reign and control of Europe. He abdicated for a second time. This time the British exiled him to the island of Saint Helena, a remote

British-held island in the mid-south Atlantic Ocean. Saint Helena was an island from which Napoleon would never escape. He lived out the rest of his lonely days on this remote island. He did have visitors, but I suspect that it was probably once or twice a year.

Napoleon died May 5, 1821 at the age of 51, and was buried on Saint Helena. He died exactly 107 years to the date of my mother's birth.

In Napoleon's rule of France, he enacted many laws that are still in use today. He built roads and improved the living conditions for the people of France. He conquered most of Europe and created a lot of enemies along the way. Hundreds of thousands of lives were lost because of Napoleon's thirst to conquer all.

The Allied victory at Leipzig strengthened Austrian Foreign Minister Karl von Metternich's hand, and in 1815 The Concert of Europe was formed. The act was dedicated to maintaining a balance of power in Europe. This cooperative effort among its members prevented any European country from gaining too much individual power and kept them from fighting one another. It worked well until the Crimean War in 1854. In the 1880s, the balance of power began to fall apart because of the ambitions of Kaiser Wilhelm of Germany.

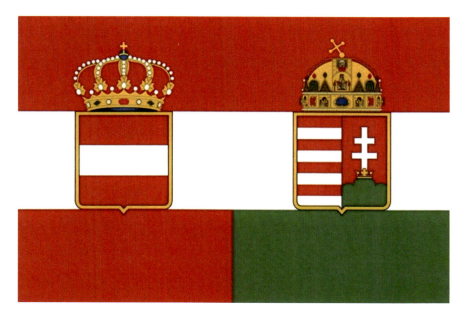

Austrian-Hungarian Flag

1867 - THE AUSTRIAN-HUNGARIAN EMPIRE

Austria-Hungary before World War I was an empire, and was the largest political entity in Europe. It spanned 700,000 square kilometres of central Europe. The empire contained within it many ethnic groups, including Germans, Hungarians, Czechs, Croatians, Italians, Poles, Romanians, Slovaks, Slovenes, and Serbs. The empire stretched from the Tyrol region north of Italy to the fertile plains of the Ukraine and far east Europe. Like its neighbour Germany, Austria was a new state comprised of many old peoples and cultures. The leader of the Austro-Hungarian empire from its inception was Franz Josef Ferdinand of Austria. He was born in Schloss Shönbrunn on

August 18, 1830, near Vienna in Austria. He divided his empire into a dual monarchy. The empire was formed in 1867 through an agreement between Austria and Hungary. It was a complicated monarchy.

The empire's political organization was unusual because of each country's origins. Franz Josef was its sovereign and emperor, though each of the two countries had their own monarchies, and each continued to exist in their own right. Both countries had their own parliaments, and some domestic self-government. There were differences between the two countries on some issues, but the empire thrived in spite of them. Both countries were overseen by a central government that dealt with matters of foreign policy, joint finance, and military command.

The central government was comprised of the two country's emperors, its prime ministers, and appointed ministers, as well as members of the military and the aristocracy. Franz Josef Ferdinand had absolute authority.

Franz Josef was a shy, sensitive man. He was hard-working and compelled by a sense of duty to his country and the empire. It has been said that he was a lonely individual, with a frozen appearance, though his facial expressions were probably misread by many of the people that met him. With the complexities of the dual monarchy and the sheer size of the empire, he had a lot to deal with. The empire's Imperial army was a large, powerful, modern one, though Franz Joseph was not a warmonger. He often rejected demands for strong action and the deployment of the Imperial army.

The Austro-Hungarian Empire brought many ethnic groups and cultures together in the empire successfully, something modern governments struggle with.

Oskar Bendl, 1902

OSKAR BENDL

My grandfather, Oskar Bendl, was born June 14, 1892 in Rybare, Bohemia, which was part of the Austrian-Hungarian empire. The Bendl family are

Austrian and dated back 236 years at the time. Oskar's father and mother, Ludwig and Anna Bendl, had nine children, three boys and six girls.

Oskar's father, Ludwig Bendl, was an extremely wealthy shipping and forwarding agent in Carlsbad, Austria. His company, Bendl Spedition and Commission, was a 125-year-old company. It owned all of the transportation in Carlsbad, as well as much of the transportation in Austria. The Bendl family also owned a large, profitable porcelain china factory in Carlsbad.

At the time, Carlsbad was a bustling city like Paris, France, with a population of about forty-two thousand people. It was a very popular tourist destination that attracted thousands of tourists from all over Europe and actors from Hollywood in the United States. It was world famous for its hot springs, as it is to this day.

Economically, the 19th century had been beneficial for the Austrian-Hungarian empire and it had expanded in banking, industry, and manufacturing. Manufacturing and industrial production increased in the western end of the empire, while the east remained its agricultural heart. The Imperial army invested heavily in railroad infrastructure, laying down thousands of kilometres of railroad tracks in and out of the two countries in the late 1800s. The railroad network was beneficial for industry and the military. Austria-Hungary's growth was the second fastest in Europe, behind only Germany.

Business was booming in these years. Ludwig Bendl's shipping and forwarding, and transportation businesses were busier than ever, and the china factory sales were booming as well. The china factory had many employees and employed over forty artisans that painted flowers, such as roses, on the fine china.

Tourists came for the hot springs in this quaint Austrian city, and wanted to take home some of the beautiful, fine china made there by one of the several fine china factories.

Life had its privileges for the Bendl family in the early 1900s. They wore fine clothes, and all of the children went to private schools, had summer vacations, and took piano lessons.

Bendl Spedition & Commission, Carlsbad, Austria 1902

*Bendl Spedition in Carlsbad's Rail-yards
foreground and right background*

Ludwig Bendl, Oskar's father, died in 1904 from a gunshot wound in a hunting accident. The bullet could not be removed. Oskar was eleven years old at the time. Upon her husband's death, his wife (my great-grandmother), Anna, decided that she and her sons would take over the family's business empire. She was a determined woman, but she had five young children at the time, and the business empire was huge. She probably did not have much of a choice in the matter, as there were probably not too many people that could afford to purchase the large businesses from her.

It was decided that Karl and Ludwig Jr. would help in the shipping and forwarding and transportation businesses when they became older. Oskar would take a supervisory position in the china factory in a few years. Anna wanted Oskar to study oil painting in London, England, before putting him among the factory's fine artisans.

Bendl China, 1920

In a few years, Anna Bendl would take up with the children's piano teacher. I suppose she had become a lonely woman, and the stress of the businesses had taken a toll on her.

At 19, Oskar went to study oil painting in London, England in 1912. He loved the arts, and the oils, having started painting at about 14.

On June 28, 1914, while Oskar was studying in England, shots were fired in Sarajevo. Assassins killed the Archduke Ferdinand, son of Karl Ludwig. The

Archduke was heir to the throne of the Austrian-Hungarian Empire. The archduke's pregnant wife Sophie was also killed. My grandfather thought, "I must go home immediately," and returned to Carlsbad in about two weeks. When he returned, Austria was in shock over the assassination.

The assassins posted themselves along the route that the Archduke and his wife would tour in Sarajevo. The tour was in an open car with virtually no security. One of the assassins threw a grenade that bounced off the car. It exploded, wounding a nearby police officer and a few bystanders. That assassin escaped.

Later that day, the Archduke decided to visit the wounded police officer at the hospital. His driver made a wrong turn along the way, and, realizing this, backed the car up. Another assassin, Gavrillo Princip, was loitering close by, and he walked up and shot Franz Ferdinand twice from a distance of one and half metres. Sophie threw herself over her husband instinctively and was also killed. The group of six assassins were all caught. One Bosniak and five Serbs that were part of The Young Bosnia Movement had carried out the assassination.

Austria-Hungary had annexed Bosnia and Herzegovina in 1908. Serbia opposed it because it allowed Austria-Hungary to distribute power and control of the Balkans. Serbia considered that a threat, and diplomatic relations between the two countries were damaged beyond repair. Princip was born to a poor family and was a Yugoslav nationalist that believed that Yugoslavs had to be united and freed from Austria.

Naturally, Franz Josef Ferdinand was furious about what had taken place. The Archduke was his great nephew. The assassination was considered a direct strike against Austria-Hungary. The Archduke was heir to the throne and he and his wife had three young children.

Sir Franz Josef Ferdinand, Emperor of Austria

On July 23, 1914, Austria-Hungary sent an ultimatum to Serbia containing ten demands.

European diplomats scrambled to diffuse the situation. Serbia, feeling assured of Russian support, accepted all the demands of Austria's ultimatum except the occupation of Serbia by Austria.

Austria-Hungary, assured of German support, rejected Serbia's response, and on July 27, dismissed warnings from Russia, France, and Britain. Britain and France feared that the situation was about to become a European war, as Serbia had already begun military mobilization. Austria-Hungary had no intentions of negotiation with Serbia. Austria Chose War.

The assassination of the Archduke was the match thrown on the powder keg that ignited World War I.

Austrian–Hungarian War Flag

WORLD WAR I

On July 28, 1914, exactly one month from the day of the assassination of the Archduke, Austria-Hungary declared war on Serbia. Russia began mobilizing on August 1. Germany demanded that Russia stop their mobilization. Russia refused to stop, and Germany declared war on Russia.

Russia's ally, France, mobilized that day, and on August 3, France and Germany declared war on each other. The German army's planned invasion of Belgium had Britain declare war on Germany on August 4, and days later, on Austria-Hungary. War erupted across Europe.

Several alliances that had formed over the past decades were invoked, and the major powers were at war. As all had colonies, the conflict would soon spread around the world. The British declaration of war was made on behalf of Britain and its dominions. Canada was one of Britain's dominions, thus Canada was immediately implicated. The war had become a World War.

World War I has been called The Great War. The war was caused by political tensions, complex military alliances in Europe, and the assassination of Archduke Ferdinand. It was the largest conflict the world had ever seen, and had the highest number of military and civilian casualties in history. It was a long, bloody war.

The armed forces—Allied and associated powers mobilized in World War I from Europe and beyond—included Russia, the British Empire and its dominions, France, Italy, the United States, Japan, Romania, Serbia, Belgium, Greece, Portugal, and Montenegro. The opposing Central powers were Germany, Austria-Hungary, Turkey, and Bulgaria.

My grandfather, Oskar Bendl, was drafted into the Austrian army, and he served on the eastern front against Russia. The Austrian army was ill-equipped for the eastern front. The Russian soldiers were very well trained and equipped. The standard Russian field guns used on the eastern front were 76.2 mm and 122 mm. They were robust enough to be used by Russia even later, in World War II.　　　[a02]

Austrian casualties were very high on the eastern front as the lines became more fragmented. Oskar told me, "The noise was deafening. Seeing fellow soldiers fall beside you that you may have talked to minutes before, were shot dead. It was very difficult." He told me, "With all the gunfire, and what was taking place, it made it very difficult to concentrate."

One must always remember that no man can dispute the honour of any man that chooses or is forced to fight for his country. My grandfather's country was Austria, and he was forced to defend it like his other countrymen.

On the battlefield, Oskar was hit by three bullets. One of the bullets remained lodged in his liver until the day he died. The war sickened him. By the end of it, he had no use for war for the rest of his life.

In 1914, Canada was an immense country with a small population of only 8 million people. At the outset of the war, tens of thousands of young Canadians rushed to enlist in the first few months "not wanting to miss the action." Canadians were patriotic and felt the war would be short, and the enemy would soon be stopped. More than 630,000 Canadians served in the war, with 420,000 going overseas. Canada and the other Allies learned, however, that they had met a very formidable force. This war would grind on for four long years.

The British government enacted The War Measures Act (WMA). Canada amended the British WMA, as the government had seen the British WMA amended numerous times. Canada introduced the Immigration Act, a "blanket act" that gave the government the power to enact "whatever law it deemed necessary." Fear and lack of understanding fed the government's paranoia. Canadians of many European nationalities and countries were deemed "aliens of enemy nationality."

Many Canadians of European descent became Prisoners of War. They were imprisoned simply because they were German, Austrian, Hungarian, Slovak, or Ukrainian. Many were accused of being spies, even though they had never returned to their homelands. Many of those that were imprisoned were born in Canada.

Over 8300 Ukrainian-Canadian men were considered "aliens of enemy nationality" during World War I, and were forced into one of the twenty-four internment camps across Canada. The two largest camps were Castle Mountain in the Rockies, and the Eaton Camp in Saskatchewan. Some internees were sent to Nova Scotia, where many of them were processed for deportation, and later deported.

On the battlefields in Europe, Canadians and the Allies were met with highly explosive shells, powerful machine guns, and poison gases. Canada also used poison gases on the battlefields. After the initial advances of the German army, the Western Front turned into a stalemate of trench warfare, the front line zigzagging close to a thousand kilometres between Belgium and Switzerland.

As the battle dragged on, life in the trenches became miserable. It was often very cold and muddy. The soldiers lived with rats, mice, and lice. Outside the trenches was called "No Man's Land." The landscape was filled with shell craters and tangled barbed wire that the Germans had put up years before the Allies arrived. The Allies had to cross "No Man's Land" to advance, and it was constantly being swept by German machine gun fire and artillery.

Adolph Hitler himself had been made "a runner" in these trenches. Hitler, and others that had become sick from the mustard gases, ran communication wires, delivered messages and ammunition throughout the German trenches during the war.

Hitler was an Austrian, and technically not allowed to join the German Army at the beginning of the war, but he managed to later.

On November 21, 1916, at the height of the war, the last significant Hapsburg monarch, Franz Josef Ferdinand, died at the age of 86. He ruled the empire for 66 years. He was succeeded by his 29-year-old great nephew, Karl I, who immediately began efforts to reform the old dual monarchy. He dismissed the head of the Austrian army, Conrad von Hotzendorff, replacing him with Arz von Straussenberg. Karl's liberalism posed a threat to the Hungarian foreign minister, Istvan Tisza, whom he would later pressure to resign in May 1917.

In 1916, Europe had been at war for more than two years. Neither the Allies nor the Germans had made any significant headway on the Western Front. The Allies planned a major attack plan in the area of Arras, France. The Canadians were tasked with capturing Vimy Ridge, about 180 kilometres north of Paris. It is a high hill, a nine-kilometre-long escarpment. The Ridge dominates the surrounding landscape on the north and east sides by the Douai plains.

The Germans had turned Vimy Ridge into a strong defensive position with tunnels, trenches, and hundreds of kilometres of barbed wire. The trenches of Vimy were manned by highly trained German soldiers with powerful machine guns. Earlier attempts to capture Vimy in 1914 and 1915 had resulted in the loss of hundreds of thousands of French soldiers.

Over one hundred thousand Canadian soldiers moved forward in the autumn of 1916. The regiments from across Canada numbered forty-two, and included the 1st Hussars and the 4th Battalion, The Royal Canadian Regiment, both from London, Ontario.

Four battalions of Canadians of the Canadian Corps moved to the front lines and formed one formation; it would be the first time they had ever fought together. The Canadians would face an even larger German army of six battalions the next spring.

Preparations for the battle were extensive and took most of that winter. The Canadians were given extensive training in trench warfare, and even raided some German positions, taking German prisoners for intelligence.

On a cold, windy night in 1917, a group of Canadian soldiers rose to check the wind, and an order was issued. The men crouched and opened valves on steel tanks in the mud, releasing poisonous chlorine and phosgene gases. In the hours that followed, the gases killed or badly injured more than 700 Canadian soldiers, their own comrades. They slowly suffocated on their own inflamed lungs or were shot by Germans as they writhed in agony.

This was Canada's horrifically botched gas raid on Vimy Ridge weeks before the more famous battle.

It was the first significant use of weapons of mass destruction on the battlefield by the Canadian Corps, and it would not be the last. Canada made heavy use of gas during the Battle of Vimy Ridge and throughout the war. Canada continued to mass produce it, and would even test it on human subjects decades later. [a03]

The Allies dug beneath German lines and set a large number of explosives under the enemy's tunnels, to be detonated when the Canadians were going to attack. Bunkers had also been built to protect the Canadian troops, and to store arms and supplies.

To soften the enemy defences prior to the attack, the Allies made a massive prolonged artillery barrage over a one week period. The heaviest shelling—with more than a million shells fired—lasted almost a week. The Canadians did that so that the Germans would not know when the attack was actually going to happen.

The Battle of Vimy Ridge began at 5:30 a.m. on April 9, 1917. It was Easter Monday. The first wave of about 15,000 Canadian soldiers attacked in the wind-driven snow and sleet. They captured enemy soldiers and artillery as they advanced, watching where the Canadian shells were hitting ahead of them. Canadian battalions in the first waves of the assault suffered large numbers of casualties. The assault on the ridge continued, and the most heavily defended ridge, Hill 145, was taken on April 10.

Two days later, the Canadian's took "the pimple," another high point of the hill.

The Germans retreated three kilometres to the east. The Allies now commanded the heights overlooking the plains, which were still occupied by the Germans. The Canadian Corps with the British to the south, had captured more ground than any previous British offensive in the war. The four-day battle at Vimy Ridge was a stunning victory, but its cost had been very high: 10,600 casualties, with 3,600 dead. German casualties at Vimy have been estimated at 20,000, with 4,100 taken as prisoners.

[a04]

Vimy was a proud moment for Canada. It was an extraordinary accomplishment, but many of the Canadian soldiers that survived Vimy Ridge, died in other battles.

Karl I's greatest efforts were directed toward ending the First World War. In April 1917, he and his foreign minister, Ottokar Czernin, visited Kaiser Wilhelm II of Germany to press for peace. The empire, they told the Kaiser, could not hold out much longer. At the same time, unbeknownst to Czernin, Karl was already in secret peace negotiations with Britain and France. Karl's wife, Zita, was French, and her brother, Sixte Bourbon-Parma, acted as an intermediary in the negotiations. The negotiations floundered when Karl refused to cede any territory to the Italians. The following year, France made the negotiations public to great effect during Germany's spring offensive in 1918. Furious with Karl's deception, Czernin resigned and the Germans never trusted the emperor again.

The unravelling alliance between the Central Powers had been pushed to the limit, but it did not break at that time. Over the course of 1918 it became clear that the tide was turning in favour of the Allies. As hunger and discontent intensified within Austria, Karl continued to press for peace, without success. In October, hoping to satisfy growing nationalist aspirations within the dual monarchy, Karl issued a manifesto establishing a federation of Austrian states. It was too little, too late. With the armistice on November 11, 1918, Karl renounced his constitutional powers.

The following March, after attempting to retain his throne, he was forced into exile in Switzerland and was formally deposed by an Austrian court. He attempted to return to Hungary several times, but was denied entrance. Karl I died penniless in April of 1922 on the Portuguese island of Madeira.

The casualties of World War I dwarfed the casualties of any previous wars. Casualties are difficult to calculate, as the heads of the new governments shifted away from those grim statistics. Many civilian and military died from diseases. Many civilians had also died from famine.

At the end of the World War I, 66,000 Canadian soldiers had been killed and 170,000 wounded. The battlefields of the Somme and Verdun were two of the largest battlefields of absolute slaughter. In a single day, July 1, 1916 the British lost 57,470 soldiers at the Somme. At Verdun there were 150,000 soldiers that were never located. A graveyard was built there in their memorial.

The Allies' military deaths of World War I have been estimated at 5,711,696, with civilian deaths at 3,674,757 people. The Central Powers' military deaths are estimated at 9,721,937 and civilian deaths are 6,821,248.

Armed forces mobilized and casualties in World War I as reported by J Graham Royde-Smith reports total casualties, Allied and Associated Powers, and Central Powers at 37,468,904. Killed and died, wounded, prisoners and missing.

(U.S. War Department February 1924)

(U.S. casualties amended by the Secretary of Defense, Nov. 7 1957) [a05]

In Austria, Anna, Oskar, and the rest of the Bendl family had survived the war.

The Treaty of Versailles—the WWI peace treaty—was signed on June 28, 1919 by the Allies and Germany. It was signed five years to the day of Archduke Franz Ferdinand's assassination. The other Central Powers each signed separate treaties, though the actual fighting had ended on November 11, 1918 with an armistice. The treaty of Versailles took six months to compile with all the negotiations and countries involved.

The Key Conditions of The Treaty of Versailles were:

- Germany was not allowed to form part of the League of Nations.
- The Rhineland was a demilitarized zone. Germany was not allowed to send any military personnel there.
- France would get the Saar (rich with coal) for 15 years and get Alsace Lorraine back.
- Austria and Germany were forbidden to unite.
- Certain rich farmlands in eastern Germany were given to Poland.
- All of Germany's colonies were taken away and given to Britain and France as mandates.
- Germany's army was not to grow bigger than 100,000 soldiers and the navy was not allowed to have any submarines and only six battleships. An air force was not allowed.
- Germany had to pay reparation costs to other countries due to damages caused by the war.

It was a bitter pill for the Central Powers. The Treaty was harsh, although many countries felt that it wasn't harsh enough. It confiscated 10% of Germany's territory, but still left it the largest, richest nation in Europe. Germany had a massive debt to repay for the war, and growth in Europe was stagnant.

In 1921, the reparation costs that Germany had to pay were assessed at a staggering $31.4 billion US dollars. The 2017 equivalent is $442 billion US dollars. Many economists predicted that the reparations were too harsh.

The Paris Treaty after World War I basically re-drew the map of this part of Europe, and new states were formed. The Hapsburg Empire ended in 1918, and The First Republic of Austria was formed in 1919. The new states that were formed included the Republic of Austria, the Republic of Hungary, and the Republic of Czechoslovakia. Austrian territory was annexed by Poland, and Hungarian territory was annexed by Rumania. The Austrian territory of the Serb-Croat-Slovene State (Yugoslavia) was annexed by Italy.

Naturally the "carving up" of the Austrian-Hungary Empire would have dismayed a lot of Austrians, like our grandfather Oskar Bendl. The proud Austrian-Hungarian Empire that he and Hungarians had known growing up was gone forever.

In Canada after the war, a large number of returning veterans had no jobs, and the economy was in terrible shape. Many of those returning soldiers looked for jobs in the factories but most of the chemical and steel plants had shut down due to low demand. This resulted in extended unemployment for the returning soldiers.

Canada's debt began before the war, but quickly escalated because of it. In 1914, a little before the war, drought caused the loss of the wheat crop. In 1914 and 1915, 50,000 railway workers lost their jobs due to Canada's railway debt. By 1918, the federal government's outlay had exceeded $2.5 million per day. In order to help pay for the war, the government introduced the sale of Victory Bonds. All of the money from the bond sales helped pay for the country's debt crises. Canada's total debt was a staggering $1,665,576,000 due to the war.

At the end of the war, Oskar married a woman and they had a child together. The child apparently had something wrong with it. Apparently, Oskar's wife took the seriousness of the child's condition so hard that she killed the baby and committed suicide.

My mother and her sisters were never able to find out much about this woman and child. We have photographs, but apparently it was never discussed with Oskar. He took his wife's suicide very hard and became a recluse. I believe the suicide haunted him for the rest of his life. The family, myself included, remembers him as a lone wolf. He painted most of the time, and only occasionally went to the taverns with his brothers or friends.

Oskar embraced the art of Alois Arnegger and Ernst Klimt, the Austrian oil painting masters of his time, and it was reflected in many of his paintings.

A year after the suicide, a friend of the Bendl family knew of another family, the Schuhmann's, who had a beautiful young daughter named Theresia. She felt she would be a good match for Oskar. The Schuhmann family were a wealthy family, of third generation weavers in Trebendorf, Austria, not far from Carlsbad.

Theresia's mother's family were the Schumachers. They were also a wealthy family and were shoe makers.

Austria is located in the alpine region of central Europe. Our family roots are in the region known as Bavaria, or The Black Forest.

The friend of the Bendl family talked to the Schuhmann family and Theresia about going to work for Oskar's mother, Anna. Theresia did not have to work but she decided that she would sew and run errands for Anna.

Very shortly, Oscar discovered this very beautiful, young woman working in his mother's home and offices. Theresia was about eleven years younger than Oskar. In 1923, Oskar and Theresia were married in Carlsbad. In early 1925, they had a child together, Ludwig Alois Bendl.

OSKAR BENDL'S BEER HALL ENCOUNTER

Oskar and his brothers and friends went to the taverns in Carlsbad for beer occasionally. The Bendl brothers came from a wealthy family, and they were outspoken, particularly Oskar. The Bendl brothers had their favourite taverns, and there were always many friends at the taverns.

One day in 1925, Oskar and his brother were having a beer in one of their favourite taverns and a frail man with pasty looking skin came into the tavern with a group of young men.

Oskar & Theresia Bendl Wedding Photo, 1923

The young men accompanying the frail man looked like a bunch of ruffians. The frail man stood at the front of the bar with his entourage of followers and in a loud voice started telling the patrons of the tavern that Germany did not have to make amends to Britain, France, or anyone else, for World War I.

Many people did this sort of thing in Austria and Germany after the war. Many Germans did not believe that Germany had actually lost the war because much of it had been fought outside of the country. The German people had not seen the damage that Germany had inflicted on the other countries of Europe.

My grandfather stood up and argued with the man with the wild ideas. The tirade ended when Oskar called the man a "crackpot"! Silence fell inside the tavern, and Oskar, his brothers, and a few others left.

A few weeks later, Oskar and his brothers were visiting another one of their favourite taverns, and the same man came in. Once again, the man recited the same speech. Oskar stood up and really laced into the man once again. It turned into a prolonged shouting match. Eventually, fed up with the man screaming at the front of the bar, Oskar, his brothers, and several of the other patrons, left. In the following weeks, the family learned that the man Oskar had argued with was Adolph Hitler. Hitler was not well known at that time, but the people of Carlsbad were becoming familiar with him very quickly.

Adolph Hitler was an Austrian, but had always considered himself a German. He also considered Austria part of Germany. There were many spies in Germany and Austria after World War One. There were sympathizers of the war and former soldiers, like Hitler, that had simply laid down their guns at the end of the war and walked away.

The Bendl's were a "God fearing family" that owned several large businesses. They did not approve of the demonstrations and speeches that were taking place in the parks and the taverns at that time. Speeches were frequent, though with only a few bystanders.

I have read many articles that have stated that the Austrian people welcomed Adolph Hitler with open arms. In the beginning, that would be stretching the truth. There were many Austrians and Germans that were very fearful of individuals like Hitler. Many people feared what those individuals might bring to their country. As well, there were people that simply went along with it, let's say, so as not to anger their friends or neighbours. I learned at a young age that when you are confronted by a snarling, snapping dog, one always speaks softly.

Oskar's mother, his brothers, and friends were all becoming quite concerned about Oskar's welfare after his altercations with Hitler. Oskar had not just argued with just any village punk, he had argued with Hitler, and he had done it more than once. There were people that were beginning to sympathize with the protesters. The Bendl family were afraid that someone would get Oskar in an alleyway and slit his throat.

Oskar's mother, family, and friends urged Oskar to flee Austria with his wife and their months-old baby as quickly as they could. Oskar and Theresia decided that Canada was probably a safe country to move to and Oskar left Carlsbad for Canada in the following weeks. Theresia stayed in Carlsbad perhaps because she felt that Ludwig was too young for the ocean voyage.

2.
JOURNEY TO CANADA

NOBEL, ONTARIO, CANADA 1926

Oskar left Austria for Canada in 1925, the ship landing at the Port of Halifax, in Nova Scotia. There he took a train to Toronto, Ontario, where he lived alone for almost one year. He would never see his homeland or his family again.

Theresia came to Canada one year later with their eighteen-month-old son, Ludwig Alois Bendl. The ship landed in the Port of Montreal. The first night of landing in Montreal, my grandmother had to sleep on hay with Ludwig. She had suffered from sea sickness the whole voyage from Europe. She told us that she remembered thinking, "To heck with this, I'm going back to Austria!"

In a few days Theresia and Ludwig were on a train, bound for Toronto, Ontario to meet with Oskar.

Theresia would never see her homeland or her family again either.

Oskar greeted Theresia and Ludwig when they arrived in Toronto. Oskar had not seen his son for over a year. In Toronto, they lived in a simple three-room apartment and talked about where they might want to live. Both disliked their concrete surroundings. They had come from a country with many large forests. I learned that their dream was to live in Berlin, Ontario (now Kitchener) to be around other German speaking people, and people from their homeland.

While they were deciding on their next move they learned of the Muskoka area, north of Toronto. Today, Muskoka is known as Ontario's cottage country. It is beautiful, rocky country, with many trees, streams, and lakes. I believe my grandparents were lured by the beauty, of Muskoka.

The Dominion of Canada offered "good, arable land" around Muskoka to immigrants in the mid- to late-1880s. They decided that "it would be tough for a couple years," but the rugged beauty of the area reminded them perhaps of their homeland. The Bendl's decided on a small town called Nobel, about 249 km north of Toronto. In 1926, they purchased a property just outside of Nobel, and they moved there that same year.

The Bendl's would learn years later, that decision would become the worst decision of their lives.

NOBEL, ONTARIO, CANADA

The History of Nobel

McDougall Township, adjacent to Parry Sound, was intended for farming. Settlers were lured to the area through the government's Free Land Grant Policy in the mid- to late-1800s. Settlers soon found that the rock and scrub bush were not suitable for farming, and logging became their livelihood. In 1907, the rail line was extended and a small train station was built seven miles north of Parry Sound. The station was named Peart, and later Ambo.

Nobel's Local History

In 1912, Mr. F. Lankford began buying land around the station. Although the true purpose was kept secret, there were many rumours about the intended use of the land, including the construction of a major ranch, or goat farm. Once 5000 acres had been secured, it was announced that Canadian Explosives Limited (CXL) had been the purchaser and they were building a dynamite and gelatin production plant on the land.

The site was well chosen. Mining operations were increasing to the north of Sudbury, the rail line was open from Toronto to Sudbury and on, water was accessible from Simmes Lake, and Georgian Bay would provide access for shipping. Parry Sound was close enough to provide a labour force, but far enough away to be protected from any explosion at the plant. Another factor was the talk of the possibility of a canal being built, connecting the Ottawa River to Georgian Bay. Building the canal would require explosives, and the company realized that if they were close to the proposed route, they would have a greater chance of being chosen as the company that would provide the explosives. The canal, however, was never built.

By 1914, the plant was completed and producing dynamite, gelatin, and cordite. Cordite is a gunpowder made from guncotton and nitroglycerine.

A village was started on the company-owned land but because the company owned the land, the town was not recognized as such. People living in the village paid rent to their landlord, CXL. The name of the town was changed from Ambo to Nobel, paying tribute to the inventor of dynamite, Swedish Scientist Alfred Bernard Nobel (1833-1896).

The plant thrived during wartime. Between 1915 and 1918, a guncotton plant, a shrapnel-loading plant, a cordite plant, and a TNT plant were built. The shrapnel-loading operation was closed shortly after it opened when a fire and explosion killed seven people. A second, larger cordite plant, built across the highway from the main operations, was owned by British Cordite Limited, but operated by CXL. After the war, the cordite, guncotton, and TNT plants were closed and the company concentrated on the production of dynamite and gelatin. In 1922, these remaining plants were closed.

FIVE ROWS OF BARBED WIRE

Canada stepped up when war was declared, supplying men in unexpected numbers while gearing up to become one of Britain's chief suppliers of armaments and raw goods. Canada had no munitions industry in 1914 and its fragile economy was in a deep recession. The conflict spurred economic growth as industries sprouted to supply Britain's insatiable demand for shells, explosives, vehicles and steel. The government agency set up to spearhead this transformation, the Shell Committee, collapsed after failing to deliver on its contracts. The better-managed Imperial Munitions Board, established in its wake, was instrumental in transforming Canada's rural economy into an industrialized one.

KEY
— Telegraph lines
— Transcontinental railways
● Munitions factories
Ocean port (size indicates total cargo volume of all sea-going ships arriving or departing in 1914, in register tons)
5 million / 1 million / 100,000
Gas - Ⓖ - ADDED BY AUTHOR

MUNITION FACTORIES WWI & WWII

MUNITIONS FACTORIES

NOBEL, ONT.
Canadian Explosives Company
This precursor of chemicals producer CIL manufactured explosives at two adjacent plants, one operated on behalf of British Cordite Ltd.

Canada's War Munitions Plants WWI & WW2 from Archives Canada

43

In 1927, the plant reopened under the name of Canadian Industries Limited (CIL) and began, once again, to produce dynamite. A new plant was constructed in 1939 on the site of the old British Cordite plant. Here, Defence Industries Limited (DIL), a crown corporation operated by CIL employees, erected buildings for the production of nitroglycerine, TNT, guncotton, cordite, nitric acid, and sulphuric acid. Up to 4,300 people were employed at DIL in Nobel. [a06]

During WWI, the government of Canada produced and tested nerve gases in the province of Alberta. Gas warfare had been outlawed by the Hague Conventions of 1899 and 1907. Canada continued the large-scale manufacture of gases, and they were used in the First and Second World Wars. The gases were sent by rail car to ports and shipped to Europe. Naturally, those rail cars passed through many provincial communities on the way to port.

The land that Oskar and Theresia Bendl purchased in 1926 was adjacent to the closed CIL property just outside of Nobel. CIL reopened the plant the very next year. The homestead (farm) was about a mile back from the highway.

There were many immigrants that worked at the CIL and the other munitions plants in those years. Oskar had worked at the CIL munitions plant for two or three years, but quit because of breathing problems. It was quite a toxic industry.

The Bendl's did not own a car. The walking distance to Nobel from the homestead was a mile. It was over six miles south on that same highway to Parry Sound.

Oskar and Theresia built a house and barn. He chopped down the trees and squared the timbers himself. I was told that Theresia helped him drag the large, heavy timbers. She sweated profusely. The cabin was fairly large and solidly built.

The soil on the farm was rocky and not good for growing anything but weeds (even they had trouble growing in the soil). Oskar would tell people years later that the family had prospered on the land. The family had not.

The Bendl Homestead, Nobel, Ontario, Canada, 1939
Hand coloured by the author

Over the next fourteen years the family grew from one child to six. Ludwig was the oldest. My mother was named Joyce-Jeanette in honour of the two French nurses that helped deliver her on May 5, 1928. Margaret was named in honour of Princess Margaret, who had visited Canada earlier in 1931. The twins, Bernard and Bernice, were born November 26, 1936, and William Ernest (Billy)—the youngest—was born in 1939. With the exception of Ludwig, all the children were born in Muskoka.

Ludwig (Louis) Bendl

FIVE ROWS OF BARBED WIRE

Joyce-Jeanette Bendl

Margaret Bendl

Bernard and Bernice Bendl (twins)

William Ernest (Billy) Bendl

Bernice, an aunt, told me that, "The neighbours' homes were very far away," and that "In the country, the only friends you have are your brothers and sisters, and all they wanted to do was fight with you!"

Oskar and Theresia Bendl became Canadian citizens on August 24, 1934.

The Bendl family had lived peacefully on this property and with their neighbours for the next fourteen years. They became poorer as the years went by.

Oskar continued his oil painting, and embraced the beauty of Canada and Muskoka, which is reflected in his paintings. He loved to paint, and painted primarily nature landscapes. He occasionally painted a scene from "the old country" until his death.

It was a large family, but Bernice has told me that she never felt like she was ever missing anything as a child, although she admits she was too young to remember.

The Bendl children did not wear shoes except in winter and when attending church. The family was Roman Catholic.

The Bendl homestead did not have hydro or indoor plumbing. They had a wood stove, used coal oil lamps, and had a water well. The family relied primarily on the food from their garden and the chickens they kept.

The Bendl's never accepted gifts from charitable organizations like The Salvation Army, their church, Star Boxes, or others, because they were too proud. The Bendl's had never begged anyone for anything, but there would be a day many years later that Theresia would beg in the streets.

The two oldest, Ludwig and my mother Joyce, spoke German. My mother, of course, learned English when she started school at the age of six. Theresia learned English quickly by talking to the neighbours, and her children when they came home from school.

All the Bendl's neighbours loved Theresia. She was a shy, soft-spoken woman. She always had a smile and a twinkle in her eye, and she always had kind words for everyone.

AN INHERITANCE FOR OSKAR

In early March, 1939, Oskar received a letter from Dr. Krizek, a lawyer in Carlsbad, stating that Oskar's mother, Anna, had died on March 9, 1939. The lawyer had been hired by the family to handle her estate. He advised Oskar to go to Shlackenwerth, Czechoslovakia, to collect his inheritance. Oskar also got a letter from his sister, Sophie, in Austria at that time, notifying him that his inheritance had been placed in a bank account and she had the receipt.

The inheritance was a huge sum of 6 million crowns. In 1939, a crown was worth about twenty cents Canadian, which made the inheritance $1.2M Canadian dollars. I had the value of that inheritance re-assessed at $20,668,421.05 CDN or 13,787,903.68 Euro on December 5, 2017 by the Bank of Canada (BOC).

That figure is what Oskar's inheritance would purchase in goods and services today. [a07]

Anna Bendl, Oskar's mother

The average yearly wage in Canada in 1939 was $956 or about 40¢ an hour. Bacon was 68¢ kg, a steak was 51¢ kg, flour was 7¢ kg, and milk was 10¢ per litre.

So, Oskar Bendl's inheritance was a vast some of money that would have helped his family considerably, to say the least.

Oskar called Immigration Canada to get a passport to go to Czechoslovakia and collect his inheritance.

Immigration Canada dragged their feet and exactly six months to the date of his mother's death, Canada followed Britain by declaring war on Germany on the eve of September 9, 1939. The declaration appeared in the newspapers the following day.

Oskar Bendl would never see his inheritance!

WORLD WAR II

World War II broke out on September 1, 1939, when Germany invaded Poland.

In 1939, Canada was a Commonwealth country controlled by the British. The country's population was primarily English, Irish, Scottish, and French Canadian. Canada's population was just over eleven million. The Liberals, led by William Lyon Mackenzie King, had governed since the 1920s.

Canada's population of Europeans had steadily increased since the mid 1800s. Germans, Austrians, Hungarians, Poles, Slovaks, Ukrainians, Italians, Japanese, and others immigrated to Canada in increasingly larger numbers during those years. In 1929 the government signed the Railway Agreement with Canadian Pacific and Canadian National Railways. It allowed the railway companies to recruit immigrants, including from the "non preferred countries" of northern and central Europe. More than 185,000 immigrants entered Canada under that agreement alone. In 1929, the government

FIVE ROWS OF BARBED WIRE

also allowed 1,300 Mennonites facing deportation from Siberia into the province of Ontario.

Not one specific historic event caused World War II. The years between the world wars was a time of much instability. The Great Depression that began on Black Tuesday, 1929, plunged the world into recession. Hitler capitalized on that economic decline and recession as he rose to power in 1933. After taking power, he established the Luftwaffe, which was a direct violation of the Treaty of Versailles, signed in 1919.

Many historians believe that the Second World War was caused by the crippling amends Germany had to pay under the Treaty. Hitler had opposed the amends many years before as he rose to power.

In 1939, the British took control of the munitions manufacturing plants in Canada. Some of the formerly closed plants were reopened, and more plants were built. Munitions manufacturing in Canada had become a "coast to coast business."

Canada, despite its vast size, had a small army, her navy was but a fleet of 15 ships, and her air force consisted of only 275 aircraft, most of which were obsolete on the eve of the European war. Despite the lack of military strength, Canada had great war potential. Canada purchased 20 million dollars of arms from the United States in preparation.

The army was the largest branch of the Canadian military at the start of WWII. It had 4,261 officers and men in the permanent army, and 51,000 in the reserves. The numbers grew dramatically over the course of the war. By mid-1942, the army had increased to over 400,000, and by the end of the war, to over 730,000 men and women.

In September of 1939, the Royal Canadian Air Force (RCAF) had 4,061 personnel, only 235 of whom were pilots. Out of the 275 aircraft available, only 19 were considered modern. The RCAF was the weakest of Canada's military branches, but that did not diminish its contribution to the war effort at the start. During WWII, Canada ran the British Commonwealth Air Training Plan, which trained 131,553 air crew, including 49,507 pilots. More than 70,000 of those trained were Canadian. By 1945, it boasted 86 squadrons and 249,000 personnel, including 17,000 women. On the civilian front, Canada produced more than 16,000 aircraft of various types. [a08]

Jack Fréchette Sr., my father, went to Britain at the age of nineteen and joined the Royal Air Force (RAF). He became a tail gunner in a Lancaster plane. He was credited for two confirmed kills, shooting down two enemy aircraft. My father told me that he was sure he shot down a lot more than two. He told me, "When the enemy fighters came after you, they came in, very fast." Of course, the gunners were targets for the fighters. Most of the Luftwaffe fighter pilots were highly skilled. The Lancaster was a slow, "lumbering giant" of a bomber with a top speed of

272 mph, making it an easy target for the faster, more agile enemy fighters.

The Avro Lancaster was considered the finest of all heavy bombers and is considered the greatest single factor in winning the Second World War. The Lancaster's dropped a total of 608,612 tons of bombs, giving it the distinction of the plane that dropped the most bombs in history. The Lancaster's armament consisted of eight 0.303-inch machine guns distributed between the nose, dorsal, and tail turrets. The bomber could carry one 22,000 pound bomb, or 18,000 pounds of smaller bombs. A total of 7,374 Lancaster's were built during WWII. Many of them in Canada at A.V. Roe in Malton, Ontario. Britain had at least 56 squadrons of Lancaster's at any given time during the war.

I asked my father why he went to Britain to fly, and he said, "I thought my chances were better." At the beginning of the war, the RAF bombers only flew at night, but that changed later in the war. The Lancaster's he flew ran sorties over Germany, dropping 4,000 lb "cookie cutter" bombs. Both of the Lancaster's he flew in were shot down returning to Britain from Germany. The second time my father was shot down, the plane had been swarmed by enemy fighters and was shot down off the Isle of Man. The plane crashed into the sea. All of the crew survived the crash, and men from the island rescued the crew using two boats.

WWII Avro Lancaster Bomber

My father suffered a broken leg. Also, the breathing passages in his throat had rotted out from breathing the pure oxygen from the flying missions at high altitudes. It was two weeks before the crew were even picked up by the British from the Isle of Man. Britain was busy running sorties with every pilot they could find. Sgt. Fréchette's tour overseas was over, and he was returned to Canada on a hospital ship.

My father did not talk much about the war, but could engage other veterans in conversation when they brought up the topic. He could "rattle off" his service number "like a machine gun." I have been told by many veterans that the airman's service number was a number that they never forgot, in case they were captured. My father knew his until he died.

I asked him if he was ever afraid, and he told me, "No, never. I actually found it fascinating flying with the British," he said.

About ten years ago, my father was on his deathbed, and I witnessed something I will never forget. He was dying of cancer and was on some drugs, though he was perfectly coherent. We were having a conversation when a male nurse of Asian descent came into the room. My father sat up, bolt straight with his arms outreached like they were on his Browning machine guns again, and in a stern voice, he shouted, "Shoot, you son of a bitch!" I was totally shocked. Was this the drugs, fear, confusion, adrenaline, or everything combined? Had it all come back to him? His response was lightning fast, but the war had ended over sixty years before, and he had not faced Japanese warplanes. The nurse was terrified and I felt very badly for what happened.

Since my father's death, I have often thought that the post-traumatic stress that many of the veterans suffer from lurks deep in their subconscious, hidden to everyone, and is more real than we can ever possibly imagine.

Most of the servicemen that went overseas were very young. Many were only nineteen and twenty years of age. They were met by an incredible war machine. Naturally, many of these young serviceman's emotions would have been overcome when they were fired on by powerful guns. The ammunition used by all the countries involved during World War II was deadly—or incapacitating, at the very least—for most of those that were hit.

Significant advances in military weapons had been made by all of the participating countries since WWI. Germany's weapons and artillery were superior at the beginning of the war. The German guns were very large and powerful. Their tanks were powerful and fast. Hitler and Germany had been preparing for war for many years.

Germany had built massive numbers of aircraft, tanks, guns, and ordinance, as competing international tensions in Europe built for years. The western nations feared the spread of the USSR and the communist state. Countries like Germany, Italy, and others rose to power to meet that threat.

CPL. Francis "Peggy" Pegahmagabow

Germany had built 119,000 aircraft in the years leading up to the war, and the wars ending.

Britain and its Allies (the United States and many other nations) also rose to the Nazi threat in Europe. They produced firearms, tanks, aircraft, and munitions in massive quantities to meet that threat. Canada's major contribution to the war effort other than its service men and women, was munitions, aircraft, and trucks. Canada alone built over one million trucks for the war effort.

Native Canadians enlisted in the militia during World War II. Many of the natives were excellent scouts and accurate shots with their rifles. One sniper that became famous was Cpl. Francis "Peggy" Pegahmagabow from the Parry Sound area reserve. He was credited and received medals for almost 400 kills. He shot and killed more people than any other Canadian in history. After the war he returned to the Anishinaabe reserve near Parry Sound from which he had come, and later became a chief on that reserve. His fellow tribesmen remember him as a hard man to deal with, being permanently altered by his experiences in Europe.

The War Measures Act of 1914 was reinstated at the outset of the World War II. German Canadians were the first ethnic group to be interned in Canada. After Mussolini's war declaration on June 10, 1940, the Canadian government gave the Royal Canadian Mounted Police (RCMP) orders to arrest Italian Canadians considered a threat to the nation's security.

Over the next five years, tens of thousands of the "new Canadians" of European and Japanese nationalities would be rounded up and sent to Prisoner of War camps and Labour and Project camps across Canada for no reason other than their nationalities. The government was fearful that those people may remain loyal to their homelands.

Veronica "Ronnie" Foster at John Inglis & Company for Bren guns, Toronto, 1940.
Library and Archives Canada

Myself and many others believe, however, that many of those European immigrants, the "new Canadians," actually were the true backbone of Canada during the war and would be for many years after the war.

European Canadians owned or worked on the farms that fed us, they worked in many of the factories, and they did many of the jobs that no one else would take. If it had not been for the sweat of those new Canadians, other Canadians would have starved to death!

Later in the war, the government would have to release many of the POWs that they had "interned" so they could work on the farms out west. Canada faced food shortages during the war. Canada's people were starving!

During and after the war, many European immigrants did not speak their native languages in public. If they did and someone heard it, people would shout "Speak English!" Many Canadians told the new Canadians to "go home." European Canadians were often called "DPs" (Displaced Persons). I remember this as a child in the early 1960s. Canadians of German descent were particularly disliked, even though many had immigrated to Canada thirty years or more earlier. Many of them had even been born in Canada.

The worst problem the government publicly had within Canada during the World War II was the conscription issue. The province of Québec opposed conscription. In 1940, the mayor of Montreal, Québec, Camillien Houde, was arrested by the RCMP under the Defence of Canada Regulations (DOCR), The War Measures Act. He was sent to a Prisoner of War camp at Petawawa, Ontario, and later sent to a Prisoner of War camp in New Brunswick. His crime was telling the young men of the city of Montreal not to enlist for the war.

Québec's current licence plate motto "Je me souviens" is from 1939. I asked Québec relatives about this motto and was told that it was interpreted by many at the time as "I was born under the lily, but I live under the rose" (the lily is Québec's flower). The direct translation is "I do remember." When asked today, people that lived in Québec during the war will say "I do remember, I will not forget"! It is not a degradation of the British. It is rather a statement of opposition to the government of Canada for its conscription and other policies during the war.

"THE LAND IS NOT FOR SALE"

In the early months of 1940, Oskar Bendl was approached by two men in suits representing the government of Canada. The men told Oskar that the government wanted to buy his land. My grandfather told them, "The land is not for sale." Once again, the two men told him that that the government wanted to buy his land. Our grandfather replied, "You make me fair offer, I will consider it."

A month later, the same two men presented Oskar with a piece of paper. He looked at it and replied, "This is ridiculous," handing the paper back to them. I was told that the offer was a paltry sum, less than what Oskar had even paid fourteen years earlier. He expected to be paid what he had paid for his land. The two men left the Bendl property.

Months later, while Theresia was shopping in Parry Sound with the twins and the baby, government agents and police stormed the Bendl homestead. Oskar was arrested, handcuffed, and taken away. He tried to explain that he opposed Nazism, that his ancestors had been allies of the British, and that they had even fought alongside them. But it was to no avail; what the government really wanted was Oskar Bendl's land.

Theresia came home shortly afterwards and saw trucks and approximately twenty men running around their property. The men were filling pails with gasoline from cans on the trucks. Theresia was shaking and in total shock. "Where is my husband Oskar?!" She screamed at the men. None of them acknowledged her. She screamed, and cried over and over again, "Where is my husband Oskar!" Three men approached her and one said, "Mam, you have half an hour to get your things out of the house."

The twins were almost four years old, the baby was in Theresia's arms. The twins were horrified and began to cry because they had never seen their mother that upset before. Theresia ran into the house and grabbed some clothing for the twins and the baby. She couldn't carry much with the baby in her arms and the twins by her side.

As Theresia and her children walked away from the house, the government agents lit the gasoline they had thrown on the house, barn, and other buildings. There was a large explosion. Theresia turned and saw her family's home and barn go up in flames.

Her mind was reeling. She was so shaken that she didn't walk to the highway, but instead, turned at the end of the lane and walked back, deep into the bush. She wandered around the bush with her children for hours.

My mother, who was twelve years old, and Margaret, who was almost ten, came home from school a short time later. They were shaken by the sight of their home burning. A government agent pointed in the direction their mother had gone. My mother and Margaret found Theresia, the baby, and the twins about an hour later. She was sitting on a tree stump sobbing. Behind them stood an old, dilapidated, abandoned lumberjack's shack.

Ludwig Bendl was working as a cook in a lumberjack kitchen a few miles away. Lou had seen the smoke earlier and rushed home when he was allowed to leave. He saw what had been done to the family's home but was able to talk to one of the men that had done some of the "work" there that day. The agent told him the direction his mother, brothers, and sisters had gone. He found them about an hour later at the shack.

The shack was small, one room shack made of barn board, with a small pot belly wood stove inside. It had previously been a summer dwelling for lumberjacks. Ludwig, Joyce, and Margaret set about cleaning out the shack. They gathered what wood they could find that would fit into the small stove. There was no hydro, water, or indoor plumbing, only a small nearby pond, which would be the Bendl family's water supply. They settled in for the night.

Two days later, Theresia walked back to her former home, hoping to salvage whatever she could. There was absolutely nothing there. Everything the family owned had been burned to the ground; it was a pile of ash. The government had even put up a fence around where the house and barn had once stood.

The government did not provide the family with any form of assistance, or even a place to live. The family had no money because the government had even looted what little money they had in their bank account. They had no clothing, furniture, or blankets. Nothing. In the months that followed, their clothing basically rotted on them.

Bernice told me they all took sponge baths with water heated on the wood stove. She told me that my mother, "Truly was an Austrian princess bathing her." She remembered my mother "washing her feet and under her arms so carefully."

The government took thousands of properties away from families who had members interned and sold many of them. They also helped themselves to the bank accounts of those families. Most often the husband was the breadwinner of the household and he had been imprisoned. The women and children of those interned were left behind and had to fend for themselves.

I estimate that over 100,000 Canadians suffered this fate during the war years. They really did suffer much more than other Canadians.

I have had people say to me, "We starved during the war, and the Prisoners of War ate better than we did." And I reply to them, "Yes, and our grandmother and her children also starved—and a whole lot more." As far as feeding the Prisoners of War, I say to them, "Yes, the government was obligated to feed them because they imprisoned them." Millions of other Canadians starved during the war, but who's fault was that?

Tens of thousands of those families wound up homeless and many thousands wound up begging on the streets. They were considered outcasts by the more fortunate people of Canada during the war.

With nowhere else to go, Theresia and her six children lived in the one room shack for about the next two years. Oskar had disappeared and the family did not even know whether he was dead or alive. Telephone calls to the government by the family to find out what had happened to Oskar fell on deaf ears. The government told them nothing. It would be almost three months before the family would learn what actually happened to Oskar.

Like spring, autumn in Muskoka brought out the mosquitoes and black-flies. The shack did not provide much protection. The bugs came into the shack between the barn boards. When it rained, it leaked through the roof. My uncle Lou chopped wood for the small wood stove as winter approached. Winters in Muskoka are cold with a lot of snow.

The family nearly froze to death in the shack that winter. The wind blew right in between the spaces in the barn board. They huddled through the nights that winter and the next, freezing in that one room shack. "By morning, a pail of water a few feet from the wood stove would be frozen solid with ice," Lou and my mother told me years later.

Joyce and Margaret had to walk almost a mile through the bush, sometimes in knee deep snow, to get a ride on the school bus to go to school. To take the Billy to the doctor in Parry Sound was an additional six miles down the highway. It was a long walk in the rain or snow. Theresia sometimes got lucky if she caught the milkman on deliveries. If she had 25¢, she paid the milkman and got a ride with him. Bernice told me the truck was not heated, and it was very cold.

The Canadian government used a food rationing system during World War II. The booklets were provided to everyone during the war, though the stamps were not adequate; anyone with a family would attest to that. There were different coloured stamps in the booklet for various food items. The booklets had stamps for flour, sugar, milk, and other foods. The food stamp booklets were distributed by the postmasters in the villages, towns, and cities across the country.

During World War II, the majority of the food that was produced in Canada was shipped overseas to feed the Canadian soldiers. Often that food was lost in transit. Many of those ships were sunk by German U-boats. They waited off Canada's coastline, and shadowed the American eastern seaboard waiting for the merchant ships as they left their ports for Europe. The Nazis had figured out they could weaken their enemy by starving them in Europe.

My father's father, Arthur Fréchette, was postmaster of Hull, Québec during World War II. Arthur Fréchette was a World War I veteran himself. He was tasked with the distribution of the food stamp booklets in that city. My grandmother, Hélène Fréchette, helped young women in Hull that had newborns, and others that had difficulties coping during the war.

Even with the food stamps there was not enough food for the larger families. Many Canadian families virtually starved during the war, including the Bendl's. Theresia even ate less, or didn't eat, so that her children got enough to eat.

Occasionally, Mr. Finch, a neighbour from a few miles away, would shoot a deer and bring the Bendl's a strip of venison. The Marchuks, whose farm had been adjacent to the Bendl homestead, would sometimes give them a bottle of milk or some butter. The Marchuks had been neighbours and friends of the Bendl's for almost fourteen years. They were

Slovaks and were very hard-working people. Their farm was very rocky, but over the years they had built a very large garden. They worked in the garden daily throughout the growing season. They were fortunate that they had a cow.

The Marchuks farm was not taken away from them, I believe, because it was far enough away from the munitions plant and didn't pose a problem for the ambitions of the CIL- DuPont company.

Joyce went to school with their daughter, Emily, and decades later, Joyce-Jeanette would become Emily's son's godmother.

News of Oskar's whereabouts came almost three months after he had disappeared.

He had been sent to a Prisoner of War camp at Petawawa, Ontario. As the family received that information though, Oskar had already been sent to another camp outside of Fredericton, New Brunswick.

In the early spring of 1941, the twins wanted to go outside to play one morning. It was cold and wet, and both children had outgrown their boots. They cried and cried. Theresia didn't know what to do, so she put on her coat and boots and walked in the slush on the highway to Parry Sound. In Parry Sound she begged on the streets for shoes or money, to buy her children shoes. Theresia cried and begged. To the more fortunate people on the street, she was just another beggar of the war. A shoe store owner learned of the woman crying and begging on the street from a customer and went to talk to Theresia. The merchant was so touched by her crying, he presented her with two new pairs of shiny boots for Bernard and Bernice.

Ludwig found out about his mother begging in Parry Sound and wasn't pleased at all. He realized that the conditions that the family faced were very grim. He headed to Toronto that spring to get a better job to help feed the family. In Toronto, he got a job as a bellboy at the Royal York Hotel and began sending money home. Ludwig had become the family leader. He was the oldest and he was the one that guided the family through the hardship of the war years. He returned to Nobel on the weekends when he was able to chop wood for the approaching winter. "I chopped wood those weekends until I couldn't lift the axe any longer," he told me. As a teenager, I remember him as a strong, powerful man with big, muscled arms.

In the spring of 1942, a man that lived in Nobel learned about the Bendl family living in a shack in the woods, and he visited them. He owned a home on the highway that had been vacated, and he offered the loan of the home for the Bendl's to live in.

The Bendl's gratefully accepted and moved in. The house did not have hydro or indoor plumbing, but it did have a big pot belly stove and a well. The house did not have any curtains, so Theresia stuck newspaper on the windows to give the family some privacy. That house also was cold, but the large pot belly stove made it livable.

They soon discovered that the house was riddled with bedbugs. Bernice told me that Theresia would often sit in their rooms at night, in the dark with a coal oil lantern. Theresia would turn the flame up on the lantern and pinch a bedbug on the mattress and flick it at the lantern. She would turn the lantern down and repeat the process again and again so her children could get a good night's sleep.

Bernice told me that she and Bernard watched their mother go to the water well from a window one day that spring. It was freezing cold and the ground was covered with snow. The well was several feet from the house and at a lower elevation. Theresia had taken two pails to fill with water. When Theresia had filled the pails with water, she started to walk up the incline and she slipped, with both pails of water landing on top of her. The young twins were horrified. Shivering and soaking wet, Theresia got up and went back to the well, refilled the pails, and successfully made it into the house.

Bernice admitted to me on a visit to Toronto about a year ago, that, though she was very young at the time, occasionally at nights to this day, she wakes up sweating and crying. She still remembers her mother falling with the pails of water that day, and she is still awakened by the explosion the day their home was set on fire in 1940. Those two horrifying events have lurked in my aunt's subconscious and have haunted her for seventy-five years. Bernice is now 81 years of age.

In 1942, Ludwig Alois Bendl changed his name to Lou Patrick Bendl. It was fashionable at the time with Hollywood and its actors like Bing Crosby and such. I suspect Lou did this perhaps to also avoid confrontation with people of British descent.

> [Author's note: The name "Alois" can be found in German, Austrian, and French names].

In 1942, Lou was drafted into the Canadian militia and went overseas for a period of two years. The Canadian government had taken the family's land and imprisoned his father, but that did not stop him from serving his country.

My mother and Lou found out thirty-eight years after the war that they had a cousin in Germany that had even flown in the Luftwaffe during the war. So basically, you had cousins fighting each other during World War II. I do know that many other Canadians had relatives overseas that fought for their countries as well.

Bernice told me that when she started school, the teacher asked each student to stand up and state their nationality. When it was her turn, she stood up and mistakenly said "German." A very loud "Ohhh!" went through the classroom. Bernice had actually been born in Canada to Austrian parents. It was a simple mistake, but it took "Many months before the other young girls would even talk to me," she told me.

People that owned a radio heard daily broadcasts about the war that caused much suspense. For the

Bendl's and many others that did not own a radio, the bits of news that they heard from others caused much suspense and anxiousness for them as well.

Hollywood and the movies kept many Canadians' spirits alive during the war. The movies gave Canadian audiences hope and kept their minds off the war while their husbands, fathers, sons, or brothers were overseas.

My mother told me once that, "if Margaret and I had a quarter of a dollar, we would sometimes walk the six miles to Parry Sound and go to the theatre for a movie. Twenty-five cents would get us both into the movie and buy a big bag of candy. We were happy." The long walk home from the movie was, of course, over six miles up McDougall Road.

Theresia and the children never stopped thinking of Oskar. Margaret told me once that, "We were always afraid that we would never see our father alive again."

In 1943, Billy was diagnosed with a Wilms' tumour, a cancer that had wrapped itself around one of his kidneys. Theresia's life had become a living hell with everything that had happened. And now her youngest had cancer. Billy cried and cried, and often asked his mother over and over again, "Why do I have to die?" It tormented Theresia and she was constantly in tears. Months later Billy was operated on to remove the kidney. The surgeons that operated on Billy botched the operation and removed the wrong kidney. One cold morning in the spring of 1943, Billy Bendl passed away "mercifully" in his sleep of pneumonia.

The living conditions for Billy had been very harsh in his very short life. He is buried in a mass grave somewhere north of Toronto because the family could not afford a grave site at the time. I have asked the Mormons for their help and possible records of his burial location. Billy Bendl would have been an uncle of ours. He was the only uncle that we never got to meet.

    The curse on the Bendl family followed them in the years ahead.

3.
CANADA'S PRISONER OF WAR CAMPS AND OTHER CAMPS

Many people don't associate Prisoner of War camps with Canada since the Canadian government has always referred to its camps as "internment camps." The government's association with the term Prisoner of War refers to military prisoners. Throughout Canadian history there have been a variety of prisons or camps built to detain people from various walks of life for different crimes.

I have discussed the term "internment camp" with other authors and a historian, and we all came to the same conclusion: Canada's so called "internment camps", actually were Prisoner of War camps.

INTERNMENT – A DEFINITION

"Internment" means putting a person in prison or other kind of detention, generally in wartime. During World War II, the Canadian government interned Japanese and many other Canadians of different nationalities in "internment camps" fearing that they would be loyal to their homelands and pose a threat to Canada.

"Internment" usually doesn't involve a trial. You are held because someone thinks you pose a threat or might be dangerous, but there is no proof.

"Internment"

(Government, Politics & Diplomacy)

a. The act of interning or state interned, esp of "enemy citizens in wartime or of terrorism suspects."

b. (as modifier); an internment camp.

The internment of tens of thousands of Canadians by the government is now considered by many to have been a big mistake. Some citizens were even detained as POWs for up to seven years. They were not traitors; most were loyal, naturalized Canadian citizens.

CANADA BEFRIENDED THEM, TURNED ON THEM, AND BECAME THEIR FOE
CANADA'S PRISONERS OF WAR

The new Canadians were arrested without committing a crime and did not get a trial. Virtually all were naturalized Canadian citizens. The new Canadians were innocent, yet they were imprisoned. All of their property was seized by the government of Canada, and much or all of that property was sold.

Canada's "internment camps" had guard towers with guards who carried rifles or machine guns. The guards had orders that if anyone tried to escape, they would be warned with "Halt or I shoot." If the prisoner didn't halt, they had orders to "shoot to kill." Because of the terms of those imprisoned and the years that they were imprisoned for a crime they had not committed, one can only conclude that they were Prisoners of War.

"Internment" is the imprisonment or confinement of people, commonly in large groups, without trial. The term is especially used for the confinement of "enemy citizens in wartime or terrorism suspects." Thus, while it can simply mean imprisonment, it tends to refer to preventive confinement, rather than confinement after having been convicted of some crime. "Interned persons" may be held in prisons or facilities known as "internment camps" in certain contexts, but also may also be known as concentration camps.

Sound confusing?

It is, though confining or imprisoning does not involve the seizure of that person's property or bank accounts, which is precisely what the Canadian government did do to the "enemy aliens." The very terms of the "internees" imprisonment parallels that of Prisoners of War and that of concentration camps, by the latter's very universal definition. "Internment" is a government's definition of imprisonment and is for them to interpret as they see fit it would appear. Make no mistake, these so called "internment camps" actually were Prisoner of War camps and will be referred to as such in this book.

The Universal Declaration of Human Rights restricts the use of internment. Article 9 states that "No one shall be subjected to arbitrary arrest, detention or exile."

World War I Prisoners of War

The War Measures Act during World War I was first introduced by the government of Robert Bordon in 1914. The Act gave the Dominion government unlimited powers to ensure that Canada was protected from any internal or external threats "that might jeopardize its ability to successfully wage war." This included banning subversive political organizations and suspending foreign-language newspapers. The War Measures Act also allowed for the internment of Canadian residents born in countries or empires at war with Canada.

The Canadian government adopted many measures by Order in Council to respond to the new exigencies of war, including the restriction of some civil liberties. Canadian authorities were given the right to arrest, detain, to censor, to exclude, to deport, to control, or capture all persons and property "considered to be a potential threat to Canada." Any resident not naturalized who had been a native of the enemy nations were considered de facto "as enemy illegal residents." The War Measures Act was subsequently approved by Canadian Parliament. The Act also authorized future actions including decisions implemented in the early days of the war by the Privy Council.

Signed in 1907, The Hague Convention guaranteed the rights of Prisoners of War held in camps. The rules of the Convention were not always or completely respected by Canada during World War I. The Convention made a distinction between Prisoners of War and civilians, but the Canadian authorities ignored that distinction to a large degree.

Over the course of World War I, a number of amendments were made to the War Measures Act. Those amendments were revised just prior to the outbreak of World War II and became known as the Defence of Canada Regulations (DOCR). This is the government refining, and doing what they deem, fitting at the time.

Canada's Prisoner of War operations during the First World War involved the arrests of thousands of civilians and genuine Prisoners of War (combatant prisoners). An order in Council of The War Measures Act required the registration, and in certain cases the imprisonment, of aliens of "enemy nationalities." The WMA included more than 80,000 Canadians who were formerly citizens of the Austrian-Hungarian empire. These individuals had to register as "enemy aliens" and report to local authorities on a regular basis. Twenty-four Prisoner of War camps were established across Canada, primarily in rural areas. The majority of the prisoners were Ukrainians that had come from the western Ukrainian lands, then held by the Austro- Hungarian Empire. The other prisoners were German or Austrian residents of Canada. There were also genuine German POWs that had been sent to Canada from England. They were all branded as "enemy aliens," stripped of what little wealth they had, and forced to work for the government. The "enemy aliens" were subjected to other state-sanctioned censures, including disenfranchisement under the Wartime Elections Act.

In 1917, with the advent of the Russian Revolution, additional regulations were added to make membership in organizations such as socialist and communist organizations illegal.

Immigration from countries that were connected directly or indirectly with the Austria-Hungarian Empire and Germany was stopped. Natives of those countries (Austria, Hungary, Germany, and the Ukraine) were classed as "enemy aliens." Those nationalities were required to carry identification at all times and forbidden to publish or read anything other than French or English. They were not allowed to own firearms or even leave the country without written permission. Many were deported.

Over 8,300 Ukrainian Canadians were forcefully moved to one of twenty-four Prisoner of War camps across Canada. The two largest and most notable camps were Castle Mountain in the Rockies and Eaton in Saskatchewan. At these camps, the POWs were forced into labour. Rich and poor, they were all thrown into the camps together. When the labour shortage began during WWI, many of the imprisoned were released into the workforce again to boost the economy, work on the farms, and support the war effort.

There is little tangible evidence of the hardship that the First World War POWs and their families endured. Many of the prisoners died of tuberculosis, pneumonia, and other diseases while they were imprisoned. Some died trying to escape the camps. Of course, the people that lived in that time are all now deceased, so that is another part of Canada's history that is hidden to most Canadians. The last camp in Kapuskasing, Ontario, closed on February 24, 1920. It should be noted that the closure of the camp was almost two years after the war.

All of the camps from the First World War have been destroyed and so have all of the government's records.

World War II Prisoners of War

Most countries have constitutions or a Bill of Rights that contain promises of what that country will provide for its citizens. As early as 1938, before World War II had even started, the Canadian government had set about looking for sites for future Prisoner of War camps and work camps. Planning began regarding the imprisonment of the "enemy aliens," including the selection of sites for the camps.

After the war started, tribunals were set up and the enemy aliens were categorized into one of three categories: A (those to be interned), B (those not to be interned, but restricted), and C (those that would be at liberty).

In October of 1939, the Canadian government in their paranoia lost all of its civility and decency, and turned its head away from its very own citizens, the "new Canadians." When World War II broke out, the Canadian government once again began imprisoning European- Canadians as they had done during World War I. Like the First World War, most were naturalized Canadian citizens. New Prisoner of War facilities began popping up across Canada and some that were used during WWI were reopened. In the months that followed the declaration of the War Measures Act, tens of thousands of Canadians became Prisoners of War.

The government of Canada invoked an amended 25-year-old War Measures Act from WWI. The WMA from WWI did not have an end date on it. Over the course of the war, the DOCR were amended numerous times. It was under the DOCR that the Minister of Justice had the ability to "intern" any individual suspected of acting "in any manner prejudicial to the public safety or safety of the state." Under this regulation, habeas corpus—the need to produce evidence against an "internee," and the right to a fair trial—were suspended.

In May of 1940, Nazi Germany had drawn the world into the war. Canada's immigration policies were discriminatory, denying entry to those seeking refuge, including Jewish peoples. Jewish families in Austria had sent many of their sons to England, fearful of them facing the Nazi death camps. Ten thousand boys were sent to England in a relief effort known as Kindertransport. England's prime minister, Winston Churchill, was worried that there could be spies. Not knowing the loyalty of Jewish boys, Britain asked several countries, including Canada and Australia, to take the ten thousand refugees. Canada was reluctant. Britain requested that Canada aid the war by taking in 2,300 civilian refugees.

England's concern prompted an order to intern all "enemy alien" males between the ages of 16 and 70 years of age. By the end of May 1940, orders were given to arrest and intern all male, and female "enemy aliens" in Canada. Camps were also built in Great Britain, the Isle of Man, Australia, Cyprus, Kenya, Mauritius, and Palestine.

Once again, many Canadians of Austrian and Hungarian descent were rounded up and sent to POW camps or labour camps. Canada was not at war with Austria or Hungary during World War II. It makes one wonder of the rationale of the decision to declare those nationalities as "enemy aliens" or "suspected terrorists." Declaring nearly 38,000 Canadians as enemies or terrorism suspects sounds a little ridiculous and far-fetched. I believe most rational people would agree that this type of thinking is called paranoia. The xenophobic government policy was justified at the time they had stated.

In 1940, an Order in Council was passed that defined enemy aliens as all persons of German or Italian racial origin who had had become naturalized British subjects since September 1, 1922 to be "interned". The government's paranoia had spread like a sickness.

LAND SEIZURES UNDER THE WAR MEASURES ACT

In 1942, the government decided it wanted 2240 acres of Indian Reserve land at Stoney Point in southwestern Ontario to establish an advanced infantry training base. The Stoney Point reserve comprised over half of the reserve territory of the Chippewa of Kettle and Stoney Point. The band members voted against the surrender of the land, but the also realized the importance of the war effort. They agreed to lease the land to the government. The Canadian government rejected the offer to lease. On April 14, 1942 an Order in Council authorizing the appropriation of Stoney Point was passed under provisions of the War Measures Act. The military was sent in to forcibly remove the residents of Stoney Point. Houses, buildings, and an ancient burial ground were bulldozed to establish Camp Ipperwash. By the terms of the Order in Council, the military could use the reserve land at Stoney Point only until the end of World War II. The military base was closed in the 1950s, but the land was not returned to the First Nations at that time.

On September 4, 1995, the First Nations started a protest in Ipperwash Provincial Park to draw attention to the decades-old land claims. They cut the fencing and drove their vehicles into the park. The Ontario Provincial Police (OPP) moved in with the hope of a peaceful end to the protests. On September 5, the Premier Harris of Ontario met with government officials to discuss the Ipperwash protest. He concluded that "the province will take steps to remove the occupiers as soon as possible."

The following Wednesday, the OPP became aware of protesters outside of the park. Out of safety concerns, they decided it would use a crowd management unit backed up by a tactical response unit to force the protesters back into the park. The tactical response squad carried steel batons, had shields, and wore helmets. The OPP intended a show of force to move the protesters. A car and a bus with protesters inside proceeded out of the park to support the other protesters in their fight. Police fired shots and three First Nations people were wounded. The family of Dudley George, one of the wounded, wanted to take him to a hospital for treatment but were detained by the police for over two hours. Dudley George died September 7, 1995 at 12:20 a.m.

On December 20, 2007, the Ontario provincial government announced its intention to return the Ipperwash Provincial Park to its original owners, the First Nations. On May 28, 2009, control of the Ipperwash Park was fully signed over to the Chippewa and Stoney Point First Nation, the rightful owners of the land. The return of the land took 64 years from the end of World War Two.

There were actually 26 documented Prisoner of War camps in Canada during WWII. They were used to imprison "enemy aliens and terrorism suspects" like Japanese or European Canadians that had been born right here in Canada. There were combatant Germans that were imprisoned in Canada during World War II as well.

In addition to the Prisoner of War camps, there were labour camps, work camps, and alternative service camps. Many of these camps are mistakenly thought of as POW camps. The labour camps, work camps, and alternative service camps held many Japanese and European Canadians, who were forced into labour. Those camps were used for individuals charged with various crimes such as resisting the war, speaking out against the crown, their nationalities, and other charges. The individuals in some of those camps were deemed as a "lower risk." The work camps were not the local jails in the cities across the country. The work camps and project camps were "detainment camps" and were used to imprison individuals charged under the War Measures Act.. They were forced into labour for anywhere from three months up to a year most often; some for up to two years. Later in the war, many others were placed in the camps for the duration of the war.

Various provincial archives list 62 project and work camps and nine other camps classified as undefined. That's a total of 97 camps including the 26 POW camps across Canada. The government, it would appear, prefers not to acknowledge those 71 other project camps in their records for some reason.

The actual number of POWs varies from book to book. My research indicates that almost 37,800 Canadians were classified as Prisoners of War. Those numbers are confusing because there were 22,000 Japanese that were detained in work camps in British Columbia alone. The Lethbridge and Medicine Hat POW camps held 15,000 Canadian POWs, combatant Germans, and Italian and German merchant marines. Years later, Camps 132 and 133 each held

12,500 POWs. There were also 24 other POW camps in Canada. So, the stated numbers seems incomplete. The actual number of POWs and all others detained has never been recorded in government documents and will probably never be known.

It should be noted that England alone had sent over 37,000 POW's to Canada during WWII.

During World War II, Canadian citizens' homes, farms, businesses, and the very traditions of their nationalities were stolen from them by the government of Canada.

The two largest POW camps in North America during World War II were both located Alberta, Canada. The United States' largest Prisoner of War camps paled in size in comparison to Alberta's largest camps..

Some of the imprisoned were considered spies because they were of Ukrainian, German, or other European descent. Many, like Oskar Bendl, just got in the government's way. The CIL-DuPont company was a crown protected corporation and they wanted our grandfather's land. A simple expropriation could have been done, but that would have taken too long, perhaps.

I believe that, because Oskar was of German descent and had come from Austria, it was just easier to lock him up and take his property.

The War Measures Act gave the authorities and its agencies the authority to take whatever action it wanted. They could arrest and hold anyone indefinitely, without reason or trial, and even deport them. There were many people that were arrested and sent to prison camps or other camps that were not considered as "enemy aliens." There were British subjects, French Canadians, Dutch, and others that also got in the way. Police agencies on all levels had the power to arrest and detain anyone without reason or just cause. There are thousands of documented cases of exactly that having been done.

CANADIAN PRISONER OF WAR CAMP LIST: WORLD WAR TWO

Camp L	Cove Fields, Québec
Camp R	Red Rock, Ontario (Fort William/Port Arthur)
Camp T	Trois Rivières, Québec
Camp V	Valcartier, Québec
Camp 10	Chatham, Ontario
Camp 20	Gravenhurst, Ontario (Calydor)
Camp 21	Espanola, Ontario
Camp 22	Mimico, Ontario (New Toronto)
Camp 23	Monteith, Ontario (also known as Camp Q)
Camp 30	Bowmanville, Ontario
Camp 31	Kingston, Ontario (Fort Henry)
Camp 32	Hull, Québec
Camp 33	Petawawa, Ontario
Camp 40	Farnham, Québec
Camp 41	Île aux Noix, Québec
Camp 42	Sherbrooke, Québec (Newington)
Camp 43	Saint Helen's Island, Québec (Montreal)
Camp 44	Grande Ligne, Québec
Camp 45	Sorel, Quebec
Camp 70	Fredericton, New Brunswick (Ripples)
Camp 100	Neys, Ontario
Camp 101	Angler, Ontario
Camp 130	Kananaskis, Alberta (Seebe)
Camp 132	Medicine Hat, Alberta
Camp 133	Ozada, Alberta/2nd Lethbridge, Alberta
Camp 135	Wainwright, Alberta

Refer to map to see locations of Prisoner of War camps and work camps.

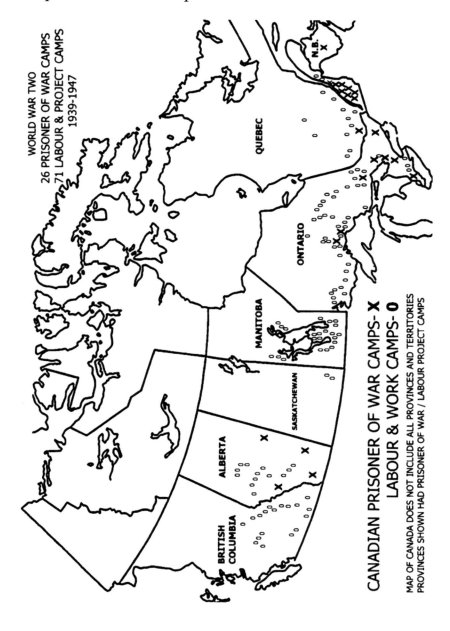

Canada's WWII Prisoner of War, Project and Labour Camps

PETAWAWA, ONTARIO: CAMP 33

In 1940, Oskar Bendl was shipped to Camp 33, a Prisoner of War camp, outside of Petawawa, Ontario. The camp was located on the Petawawa Forestry Reserve. It was occupied by militia in times of peace. When the war broke in 1914, it housed 750 German, Austrian, and Italian POWs. The Petawawa POWs were "employed" in road cutting, timber felling, and ground clearing. The camp closed in May 1916.

Camp 33 reopened in May 1939, and temporary camps were set up in Old Fort Henry in Kingston and also in the Citadel in Québec City. Most of those imprisoned in Canadian camps during WWII were Germans, of German descent, Italians, or Japanese. In mid-December of 1939, POWs from Canada's east coast, Québec City, and Kingston, Ontario were transferred to Camp 33. In 1941 alone, 756 captured German sailors were sent to Canada. Many of those sailors wound up at Camp 33.

Exile took two forms for the many imprisoned during World War II. There were relocation centers for families and relatively well-off individuals who were considered a low security threat; and there were Prisoner of War camps for single men, those less well off, and those who were deemed to be a higher security risk. Between 1939 and 1945, 850 German Canadians were accused of being spies for the Nazis, as well as subversives and saboteurs.

By the middle of December 1939, all of the POWs from Canada's east coast and Québec City were sent to Camp 33 by train. Prisoners from Kingston were sent there by bus, escorted by the Ontario Provincial Police (OPP). The Canadian government declared war on Italy on June 10, 1940, and designated Italian nationals and Italians naturalized after 1922 as "enemy aliens."

Camp 33 prisoners were all men, there were no families in that camp.

At Petawawa, our grandfather met Camillien Houde, the mayor of Montreal, and they became best friends. Camillien Houde was an educated man and was the last of a generation of a family from Paris France.

During World War II, Italians were sent to three POW camps: Kananaskis, Alberta; Petawawa, Ontario; and Fredericton, New Brunswick. In a few months after arriving at Petawawa, Camillien and Oskar would be shipped to Ripples, outside Fredericton, New Brunswick.

CAMP B70 RIPPLES FREDERICTON, NEW BRUNSWICK
FIVE ROWS OF BARBED WIRE

I named this book *Five Rows of Barbed Wire* because Camp B70 Prisoner of War camp had the distinction of having five rows of barbed wire on its perimeters.

OSKAR BENDL
Fredericton, New Brunswick
October 16, 1942
PENCIL DRAWING BY INTERNEE GLASSER

Oskar Bendl POW, 1940–1943

Located about 34 km east of Fredericton, New Brunswick, Ripples was the most eastern Prisoner of War camp in Canada in World War II. It is about 8 km from the town of Minto. It is pretty rough country. Camp B70 was called Ripples by the prisoners, their families and the locals at the time.

The site of this camp was likely chosen by the government because of its remoteness. The area was heavily forested and surrounded by many swamps. The black-flies, mosquitoes, and deer flies were plentiful and were a nuisance to the prisoners spring through fall.. There were plenty of trees for the enslaved prisoners to cut.

It was an ideal place to keep prisoners because it deterred them from escaping. If a prisoner did escape, they would likely have been eaten alive by the aforementioned pests

Most people in the Maritimes had no idea that there was a POW camp in their province.

Camp B70 covered 58 acres, which included a 15-acre fenced in compound. It is one of the 26 Prisoner of War camps in Canada, and was the only one in the Maritime provinces during World War II. From 1940 to '41, it was home to German and Austrian Jews whom had escaped the brutal holocaust of Nazi Germany and fled to England. Winston Churchill, not knowing the loyalty of the Jewish people, asked Canada and Australia to house those refugees. Seven hundred and eleven Jewish Prisoners of War were sent here. A year and a half later, Britain decided that many of the Jews that had been sent here could contribute to the war effort. They were given the opportunity to return to England and join the military or find a sponsor and remain in Canada. Many of the Jewish peoples' contributions in those years go beyond that of the war effort, and were also in science, medicine, and business.

The camp was closed for three months for construction that would allow for a larger and more diverse group of prisoners. In Phase II of the camp between 1941 and 1945, the camp became a Prisoner of War camp for captured merchant German and

Italian marines, Canadians, and those who had spoken out against the war or supported Germany.

Prisoners often tried tunnel escapes, but the tunnels collapsed when the heavy prison trucks drove on the perimeter roads around the camp. The most popular type of prison escape attempts was when the prisoners went into the forest to cut wood. It was a game to see if the guards would notice. They were usually caught within minutes. If they did manage to make it deep into the woods, they would be found the next day, cold and—I am sure—very sore from the bug bites. The prison's population was men, but, like several other of Canada's camps, there were boys as young as 16 years of age that were imprisoned.

Upon entry to the camp, prisoners were told by the camp's commander that if they tried to escape, they would be warned and then they would be shot. He went on to say, "We really don't like shooting prisoners." The perimeter of Camp B70 had five rows of barbed wire. In the corners of the compound, the barbed wire intersected and was "knitted" in a web-like fashion, making it impossible to escape. The rules of the camp were posted on steel bulletin boards in each of the barracks in the camp.

KRIEGSGEFANGENE LAGER "B" CANADA
(POW CAMP B CANADA)

BEKANNTMACHUNG
(BULLETIN)

1. IT IS STRONGLY FORBIDDEN THAT YOU MUST NOT GO 25 FT. (9 METERS) CLOSE TO THE BARBED WIRES OF THE CAMP FENCES.

2. IF YOU DO NOT OBEY THE COMMAND "HALT OR I'LL SHOOT," WE SHOOT.

3. WHEN A PRISONER IS CALLED, HE MUST STOP, RAISE HIS HANDS, AND WAIT FOR HIS GUARD TO GIVE HIM ORDERS.

4. ALL BRITISH OFFICERS MUST BE GREETED WITH THE UTMOST RESPECT.

5. ALL PRISONERS WILL LIVE IN BARRACKS. A MEMBER OUT OF EACH BARRACK IS TO BE ELECTED TO SUPERVISE THE OTHER MEMBERS IN THE BARRACK AND TO REPORT TO THE COMMANDER OF THE CAMP IN CERTAIN CASES. THE SUPERVISOR IS ALLOWED TO BE CHANGED WHEN HE WANTS, BUT THE COMMANDER MUST APPROVE.

6. THE MAIL AND PARCELS FOR THE PRISONERS WILL BE MADE KNOWN IN A FEW DAYS.

7. PRISONERS WILL GET THEIR STRENGTH BY TALKING ABOUT THE WAR.

8. MISBEHAVIOR IS DEALT WITH BY STRICT PUNISHMENT.

CAPTAIN W.S.P. GOW, ADJUANT
POW INTERNMENT CAMP
12 AUGUST 1940

Camp bulletin boards for prisoners

The guards of the camps were veterans of the First World War who had enlisted for WWII, but were denied active duty. They were put on the Veterans Guard Roster. There were 350 guards at any given time. They were rotated periodically among the other 25 camps in Canada to prevent familiarization with the prisoners.

The prisoners wore a blue denim jacket and trousers. The jacket had a 15 cm red dot on the back. The back of the jacket had a circle cut out of it and the red fabric had been sewn in. Naturally, the red fabric could not be removed without destroying the jacket. The denim trousers had a red stripe down the right pant leg. The prisoner's denim hat also had a red stripe on the top as well. It was a highly visible uniform, and of course made the prisoner an easy target.

The prisoners worked mainly in the forest, logging. They were required to cut 2,500 cords of wood each year to heat the 100 wood stoves in the barracks during the colder months and for cooking purposes. The prisoners were organized into work crews, and were paid a "slave wage" of 20¢ a day in POW money for their hard work. In 1940, the average Canadian hourly wage was 40¢. Prisoners that refused to log were assigned to latrines, cleaning, and other undesirable duties. The POW money was held by the canteen officers. The prisoners could spend their "slave wages" on cigarettes, pipe tobacco, chewing gum and other sundries in the canteen.

They could also order certain items from the Eaton's or Sears catalogues.

The POW money system is believed to have been used to prevent money from being stolen from fellow POWs. It also prevented an escaped POW from purchasing street clothes and transportation in an escape attempt.

Canadian POWs were allowed to send letters for free and receive one package per month.

I have been fortunate enough to meet a few of the last aging surviving sons of former Prisoners of War. I have collected their thoughts as handed down by their fathers. I am left with the feeling that their families were also deeply hurt by their fathers' imprisonment.

Wolfgang Preussner, son of a former Ripples POW, told me that his father said, "It was always stressful. The guards in the towers had guns and they were always pointed at you and the grounds. It was horrible." His father said, "I had done nothing," and "You made sure you never angered a guard for fear of reprisal."

Gunther [last name withheld], the son of another former POW at Ripples, told me his father said, "Most of the guards and prisoners got along well, but there were guards that you had to tiptoe around." His father had told him that "Many of the prisoners gave the guards things such as carvings that they had made in order to stay friendly and keep the peace with the guards."

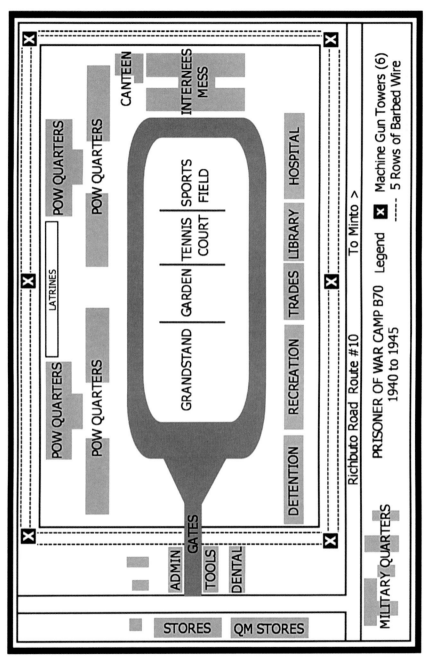

Camp B70 Ripples Layout
Drawing by the author

Both men told me their fathers thought the food was not good. They also said, "There was no shortage of food, but the food in the camp was awful."

Many of the prisoners in the camp were very skilled or talented. There were teachers, plumbers, mechanics, doctors, and many others that were skilled. The prisoners were asked on occasion to do work in homes and offices in Fredericton. Many of them gladly did the jobs to escape the drudgery of the camp.

Besides the skilled trade POWs, there were many skilled whittlers, carvers, oil painters, water colour artists, pencil sketchers, and many others with various skills. The craftsmanship of many of those prisoners is astonishing. One of the oil painting artists at Ripples was Oskar Bendl. He ordered supplies of board, oil paints, and brushes from the T. Eaton catalogue, paying for the supplies with his POW money at the canteen. When his order arrived, it was inspected before the prisoner received it, just like the other inmates' orders. That often took several days.

Oskar did a little whittling occasionally, but "oil painting ran in his blood." He often gave paintings to other inmates that he had built a rapport with.

Restlessness was common in the crowded camp. Being cooped up with a thousand prisoners in a fifteen-acre space gave many of the men a feeling of hopelessness. Unlike someone in a public jail, they did not know when they were going to be released.

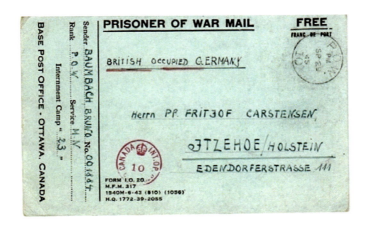

Prisoner of War Index Card
Courtesy of Ted Jones

Prisoner of War Mail Postcard

FIVE ROWS OF BARBED WIRE

There were others that were thankful to be in the camp. Helmut Kallmann was one of 500 Jewish prisoners in the camp. He knew that his life could well have ended, like other members of his family, in the death camps of Nazi Germany. Mr. Kallmann had been a POW in England before being sent to Canada. He was 16 years of age when he was imprisoned at Ripples. In the early days of the camp, the barracks were not even heated. When the government of Canada released the Jewish prisoners in 1941, many went to join family in the United States. Several, like Mr. Kallmann, stayed in Canada. Many of those former Jewish prisoners made great contributions to Canada after the war, and many attained positions of responsibility and became leaders in their respective fields. After the war, Mr. Kallmann managed to locate over 100 of the former prisoners. There were some that had no desire to revisit the past, but there were several who were pleased to hear news from old friends. [a09]

My grandfather passed his spare time over the next three years painting and socializing with Camillien, a Mr. Koenig from Toronto, and others. Oskar painted some fifty paintings while he was at Ripples and gave them to the other prisoners, or traded for sundries that he required. I have been told that the families of those POWs that have Oskar Bendl paintings cherish them to this very day. I learned from family members that Oskar gave painting lessons to other aspiring artists while he was at Ripples. The

New Brunswick Internment Camp Museum's arts section that opened in Minto, New Brunswick in 1997, is dedicated in Oskar Bendl's name. Joyce and Lou were also honoured with museum ribbon cutting ceremonies at the opening.

If you should look up Oskar Bendl in the Library and Archives Canada, Thematic Guides, you'll see that the government spelled his name incorrectly and listed the time period he was imprisoned incorrectly. His name was Oskar by birth, not Oscar. And he was not imprisoned from 1940–1945, it was 1940–1943. This is one example of unreliable bookkeeping on the part of the Canadian government.

Bendl, Oscar.   1940/10-1945/11. File

RG117-A-3.

Textual records. [Acess: Restricted by law]
Government

Finding aid number: 117-15
Show all 1 results from Archives

Information on Oskar Bendl Restricted
Govt. of Canada Archives

No records on Oskar Bendl or any other prisoners are available if that prisoner received medical services while imprisoned. I cannot feel anything but amused by this government ruling. A good number of the POWs most definitely required medical services at some point while they were imprisoned.

Canada did not have a Privacy Act in those years. Oskar was imprisoned seventy-five years ago and has been deceased for over 52 years. So, the government's ruling makes information unavailable to anyone, including grandsons, great grandsons, and possibly great-great grandsons.. Are they trying to hide something, or is this ruling meant to significantly lower the work volume for government workers today?

In the spring of 1943, Oskar received letters from Theresia telling him of Billy's death. Oskar became restless and more depressed in the following weeks.

Meanwhile, elsewhere in British Columbia and Alberta Canada tens of thousands of people had been sent to Internment camps, Project camps, Labour Project camps, and relocation centres.

I wanted to mention these camps and the Alberta POW camps as they were the largest camps in North America. The United State Prisoner of War camps paled in size to the western Canada camps.

JAPANESE PRISONER OF WAR CAMPS IN BRITISH COLUMBIA

The largest single nationality group imprisoned in Canada during World War II were the Japanese Canadians in the province of British Columbia.

Immigration from China and Japan began during the Fraser River gold rush of 1858, and by 1910 East Asians constituted 10 percent of British Columbia's population. In 1880, at the insistence of the provincial government, Ottawa imposed a head tax of fifty dollars on all Chinese immigrants; this tax would expand to $500 in 1923 and would remain in play until 1930. Despite authorizing the tax, the federal government acted as a brake on local discrimination against Asian immigrants. In 1900, 1903, and 1905 when the BC government tried to introduce English-language requirements in hopes of curtailing Chinese immigration, Ottawa frustrated its efforts on the grounds that it, not Victoria, had jurisdiction over immigration. The Chinese were also denied provincial franchise, and though they were permitted to vote federally, Ottawa based its list of electors on that of the provinces, which effectively denied all voting privileges to the Chinese in British Columbia. Once the Japanese population started to exceed that of the Chinese in the 1930s, legislators focused on curbing its influence in the province. In 1928, Japan agreed to limit its emigration to 150 people per year. After years of encouraging racist policies, the provincial branch of the Trades and Labour Congress and the Co-operative Commonwealth Federation (CCF) called upon the provincial and federal government to enfranchise Asian residents. A partial success won the vote for Japanese veterans of the First World War, but, learning from this experience and wishing to avoid setting a precedent, the Liberal government exempted all citizens of Japanese descent from military service. These developments created the context

FIVE ROWS OF BARBED WIRE

for the evacuation and deportation of all Japanese Canadians. [a010]

During the Second World War, many British Colombians became fearful of the Japanese people living in the province. They believed that the Japanese posed a threat to Canada and wanted the provincial and federal governments to rid Canada of them. The Liberal federal government and then Prime Minister Mackenzie King wanted the British Columbian's votes. Since the Japanese were outnumbered by the other nationalities, the Mackenzie King government was eager to help out. In the beginning, all Japanese males between the ages of 14 and 45 were ordered to the camps 160 km inland. They had not committed a crime; they had faced a racist Canadian populace. The homes and all property of those Japanese Canadian citizens were confiscated. The order was to "safe guard" the Pacific coastline from Japanese spies.

All Japanese fishing fleets were taken and their owners were sent inland to imprisonment. The Japanese Canadians were sent to one of eight camps in the British Columbia interior.

The war caused large labour shortages for farmers, especially the sugar beet farmers. The Security Commission Council organized sugar beet projects to combat the labour shortage. This gave the Japanese a choice: work in road camps as slaves or go to the beet camps and be with their families.

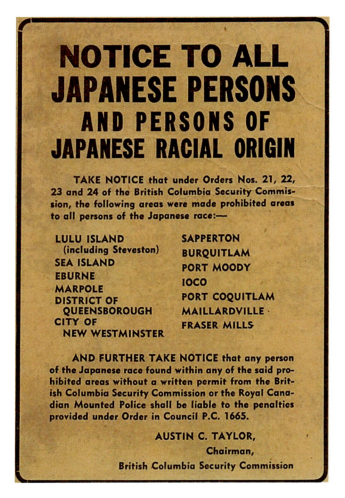

British Columbia Security Commission, Japanese

Over the course of the Second World War, almost 22,100 Japanese men, women, and children would be forcibly moved from the British Columbia coastline to the interior of the province. Their homes, businesses, and all property was confiscated and auctioned off or sold by the Canadian Custodian of Aliens. This included homes, farms, clothing, furniture, and other possessions. The items were sold cheaply and quickly.

The money collected from the sales was used to pay the auctioneers, realtors, storage, and handling costs. The money that was left over was used by the government to cover the costs of the POW imprisonment.

> [Author's note: Under the Geneva Convention, Prisoners of War did not have to pay for their imprisonment. The government of Canada did not follow the Geneva Convention's rule.]

Toyo and Kosaburo Takahashi were model citizens of Victoria, BC. Their award-winning garden at 42 Gorge Road was a local tourist attraction, and even caught the attention of the visiting King and Queen in 1939. The Takahashis, a Japanese Canadian family, fund-raised for local charities, and when war came they led efforts to sell Victory Bonds to the city's Japanese Canadian community. When evacuation was ordered, they dutifully paid their own way to Toronto. "Please remind yourselves that before oppression became politically fashionable...the Japanese minority had the best reputation for morals and for civic spirit of any minority in British Columbia," Toyo wrote a 1944 letter. "This property is our home, our reward for long years of toil...a stake in the future of Victoria."

The Takahashis never returned to Victoria. Their beloved house, and whatever gardens remained, were forcibly sold off to William and Gladys Henney for $10,000 ($136,250 in 2017 dollars) on June 13, 1946.

Imperial Japan had surrendered 10 months earlier and much of Canada's Second World War army was demobilized. Still, nearly two years after the Takahashis had begged to keep their home, the Dominion government was busy selling it off anyway. The restrictions of internment were not fully lifted from Japanese Canadians until 1949. [a011]

> [Author's note: The value of the Takahashis home in 2017 dollars is not representative of its real estate value in 2017.]

AN APOLOGY TO THE JAPANESE CANADIANS

20th Anniversary of the Canadian Government's Formal Apology for Japanese Internment during World War II

Shortly after Japan's entry into World War II on December 7, 1941, Japanese Canadians were removed from the west coast. "Military necessity" was used as justification for the mass removal and incarceration despite the fact that senior members of Canada's military and the RCMP opposed the action, arguing that the Japanese Canadians posed no threat to security.

In 1942, Japanese Canadians were to leave the "restricted area" and be moved inland 100 miles (160 km) under the authority of The War Measures Act. The order affected more than 21,000 Japanese Canadians. Many were first held in the livestock barns in Hastings Park (Vancouver's Pacific National Exhibition grounds) and then were moved to hastily-built camps in the BC interior. At first, many men were separated from their families and sent to road camps in Ontario and on the BC/Alberta border. Small towns in the BC interior, such as Greenwood, Sandon, New Denver, and Slocan became internment quarters mainly for women, children, and the aged. To stay together, some families agreed to work on sugar beet farms in Alberta and Manitoba, where there were labour shortages. Those who resisted and challenged the orders of the Canadian government were rounded up by the RCMP and incarcerated in a barbed wire Prisoner of War camp in Angler, Ontario.

Despite earlier government promises to the contrary, the Custodian of Enemy Alien Property sold the property confiscated from Japanese Canadians. Unlike Prisoners of War of enemy nations who were protected by the Geneva Convention, Japanese Canadians were forced to pay for their own internment. Their movements were restricted, and their mail censored.

In 1944, under intense pressure from government officials, many Japanese agreed to repatriate to Japan. But when Orders in Council were finally passed in 1945, thousands applied for cancellation. The Mackenzie King government initially refused to rescind the Order, but following a failed court challenge to the Judicial Committee of the Privy Council in London and a massive lobbying effort by various advocacy groups, including civil liberties associations, it agreed in 1946 to do so.

On December 15, 1945, cabinet passed Orders in Council PC7355, PC7356, and PC7357 to send 10,347 Japanese Canadians to Japan. Three quarters of them were Canadian citizens, and half of them were Canadian born. Civil libertarians moved into action, opposing the government's movements.

As World War II was drawing to a close, Japanese Canadians were strongly encouraged to prove their "loyalty to Canada" by moving east of the Rockies immediately, or by signing papers agreeing to be repatriated to Japan when the war was over. Many moved to the Prairie Provinces, others moved to Ontario and Québec. About 4,000, half of them Canadian-born, one third of whom were dependent children under 16 years of age, were exiled to Japan in 1946.

In September 1988, the government of Canada formally apologized to the Japanese Canadians in the House of Commons, and offered compensation for wrongful incarceration, seizure of property, and disenfranchisement during WWII.

"I know that I speak for Members on all sides of the House today in offering to Japanese Canadians the formal and sincere apology of this Parliament for those past injustices against them, against their families, and against their heritage, and our solemn commitment and undertaking to Canadians of every origin that such violations will never again in this country be countenanced or repeated."

[Prime Minister Brian Mulroney's remarks to the House of Commons, September 1988]   [a012]

[Author's note: Though I cannot speak for those Japanese Canadians, I do not believe the apology eased the pain or suffering. Also, the apology had come forty-three years after the war. Most of those Japanese Canadian former Prisoners of War were already deceased by then.]

The prime minister's apology fell short that day. No apology was offered to the almost 16,000 Austrian, Hungarian, Italian, German, Slovak, Ukrainian, and other European Canadians who had also been Prisoners of War.

THE TWO LARGEST PRISONER OF WAR CAMPS IN NORTH AMERICA

Camp 133: Lethbridge, Alberta

The Lethbridge and Medicine Hat Alberta Prisoner of War camps were the largest in North America, vastly outstripping the largest camp in the United States.

The original camp in Lethbridge operated between September 30, 1914 and November 11, 1916. Originally the camp operated in the poultry buildings of the Lethbridge Fair Grounds. The detention centre was called "The Chicken Coop." The prisoners were Austrian, German, and Turkish reservists. There were other Canadians that were imprisoned because they "sounded like they may be German" or others that had spoken out against the crown (uttered anti-British statements). The Lethbridge camp was close to the American border, and many of the prisoners lived in southern Alberta. There was a great incentive to try an escape, and many were shot in that pursuit. The camp was closed in 1916 and the inmates were sent to other camps for the duration of the war.

When World War II was declared in 1939, "suspected enemy aliens" were again rounded up as they had been in WWI. Those suspected of ties to the Nazis were sent to camps at Kananaskis, Alberta, and Petawawa, Ontario.

In 1942, prior to the Lethbridge and Medicine Hat camp openings, the Allies defeated German Forces in north Africa. Ten thousand German Prisoners of War were shipped to New York and transferred by the Canadian Pacific Railway to the Ozada camp in Alberta.

FIVE ROWS OF BARBED WIRE

They lived in tents until the larger camps at Lethbridge and Medicine Hat were complete.

Lethbridge Camp 133 was built in the summer of 1942 and re-opened to house prisoners temporarily at Camp Ozada, a summer tent camp west of Calgary. By November of 1942, 1,341 POWs were moved to Lethbridge. There were 22,000 prisoners at Lethbridge and Medicine Hat. In time the population of the two camps hit 12,500 each. The Lethbridge camp was divided into six sections, each with mess halls, kitchens, entertainment facilities, and six dormitories. The prisoners there were allowed to do the cooking. Meals were given in shifts due to the large number of prisoners. The food was standard rations that the Canadian armed forces ate.

Other non-combatant prisoners engaged in their professions as doctors and dentists. There were prisoners that cut hair, repaired shoes, and provided other services.

As in the other provinces in Canada during the Second World War, there were shortages of men to work on the farms. Canada had sent many young men off to war and many other young men had been made prisoners of war. The people in Canada were starving. Sugar beet farmers requested labour assistance from the government and the camps. By 1943, an agreement was reached and some of the prisoners worked on farms in southern Alberta. Some of the prisoners worked on the farms during the day and returned to the camps at night, others that worked on the more distant farms with less supervision were kept in lodges. The prisoners that worked on the sugar beet farms were paid 50¢ a day. Prisoners that worked in many of Canada's other Prisoner of War camps worked for 20¢ a day. The Japanese Canadians were not paid.

In December 1946 the camp was closed.

Camp 132: Medicine Hat

The Medicine Hat Prisoner of War camp was the second largest POW camp in North America. Camp 132 opened in 1943, and spanned 50 hectares. The camp was built for a capacity of 12,000 prisoners—a significant number, as the population of Medicine Hat was 12,000. In 1943, Britain was fearful of an invasion and sent over 37,000 Prisoners of War to the more remote camps of Canada.

Camp 132 held many high ranking Nazi officers, and there were often conflicts with lesser members of the SS. The camp operated within the hierarchy of the German officers. There were often fights, and there were at least two murders at the camp. A subsequent investigation by the RCMP sent several of the POWs to a Northern Ontario lumber camps. Six of the POWs were returned to Medicine Hat, and tried in the Medicine Hat civilian courthouse. Five were later hung in the Lethbridge jail.

In the camps across Canada, more than 140 combatant prisoners died between 1939 and 1940. Hundreds of others died from disease, heart attacks, strokes, cancer, and falling trees when logging. At the request of the German War Graves Commission, the remains of the combatant Germans were sent to a German war graves section in Kitchener, Ontario for burial. It was considered easily accessible to relatives who might want to visit the graves. Some of the less hard-line prisoners from the Medicine Hat camp were allowed to work on the farms outside the camp.

Escape attempts were made at Lethbridge and Medicine camps like the other Prisoner of War camps. The prisoners were generally younger and in better shape than their guards. Often, it was a game to see if their captors would notice.

One POW, Franz von Werra, a celebrated German fighter ace that had been captured in 1940, jumped off a train carrying himself and other POWs to Ontario. von Werra crossed the St. Lawrence River into New York state and successfully made it to Mexico and South America. Eventually, he managed to return to Germany.

von Werra was decorated by Hitler on his return to Germanyy. He rejoined the Luftwaffe and died in October 1941 when his plane crashed into the North Sea.

After the war, all of the combatant prisoners were returned to their newly partitioned country. In the years after the war, many of those former German Prisoners of War would immigrate to Canada with their families. Many felt that they had been treated very well by their captors, and decided Canada was a nice place to live.

4.
OSKAR BENDL'S RELEASE AND A LONG WALK HOME

In the summer of 1943, Oskar was released from the Ripples Prisoner of War camp. No one knows why. What we do know is that his morale was quite low. As mentioned, he had received letters telling him of his youngest son's death. It is not known whether he was released for humanitarian reasons, or the authorities had figured that there was no longer any reason to hold an old man for not surrendering his property to the government.

Oskar's friend Camillien Houde was also released about that time, and returned to Montreal where he was greeted by a roaring crowd of almost fifty thousand people. He ran for mayor again and was re-elected.

Oskar did not have enough money to even take the train home. He had worked for the "slave wage" of twenty cents a day for years. He decided to walk home.

Oskar knew that most Canadians hated the Germans during the war. He spoke with a heavy German accent and—as he told the family later—he was afraid he would get "roughed up or even worse" if he walked. He walked from the prison camp in Ripples, New Brunswick all the way home to Nobel, Ontario. The distance in 1943 would have been greater than it is today with the modern highways. Today, that distance is 1,632 km (1,056 miles) via #401 and AutoRoute 20. That is greater than the distance from London, Ontario to Marietta, Georgia in the southern United States.

Oskar walked in the mosquito-infested nights, and if it rained he walked in the darkness in the rain. During the days, he slept in the ditch or on the edge of farmer's fields. He told Lou that if he got lost he would sometimes stop at a farm house in the early evening to ask directions if the farm looked like it might be owned by Europeans.

Lou told me that no one knows what Oskar ate during his walk home. He probably ate the berries along the edge of the highway or what he could find on the edge of farmer's fields. It is not known how long it took him to walk to Nobel. Oskar lost track of the number of days he walked. Surely, it would have taken him over a month, probably much longer.

Oskar reached just south of Nobel in the middle of the night. On the edge of the highway he looked in on a farm house that he had known the owner of years before. There was a light on in the farmhouse. Oskar cautiously walked up the lane way and knocked on the door.

The owner opened the door and recognized him immediately, though Oskar had become frightfully thin. Oskar asked the owner of the farm if he knew of his family's whereabouts. The man told him that the family had moved into a house just four miles north on that very same highway. Oskar thanked the owner of the home, resisting an offer for him to come in and rest for a bit.

I believe he was so invigorated by the fact that he was so close to home and being with his family, that he had to keep moving that night. In a matter of an hour or so, he could be with his family again. Oskar reached the house, but there were no lights on. He walked up the short lane and banged on the door. A couple of minutes later a lantern was lit inside the house and Theresia opened the door. Minutes later, Joyce, Margaret, Bernard, and Bernice were all in the kitchen hugging. Bernice told me that she and Bernard did not even know that Oskar was their father because he had been gone so long and was very skinny. In the hours that followed, she told me, they learned that the man was their father. Bernice told me "We were up the rest of the night. We hugged and kissed and cried all night long."

Bernice told me that Oskar had begun throwing up a lot of the time, and it made her and Bernard sick to see it. Oskar was very thin and haggard looking. Ripples, the logging, and the very distance he had walked took a huge toll on him. It took several months for Oskar to regain his health.

When Oskar regained his health, he told the family "There was no way that the family could remain in the Parry Sound area given the black mark that the government had set upon the them by his imprisonment." The Nobel/Parry Sound area was primarily British, though the rural area did have many European settlers. But the Bendl's property had been taken away from them.

Once again, Oskar hit the road. He walked from Nobel to Toronto to get a job to feed his family. He walked at night and slept in the ditch during the day as he had done before. In Toronto, he got a job at St. Michael's Hospital, where his primary duty was burning bandages. Shortly after, the family packed their bags and moved to Toronto.

In Toronto they lived on Richmond Street. In the early 1940s, this area was not really a desirable part of Toronto. There was a large parking lot across the street where truckers slept in their trucks. Prostitutes frequented the area and were always "plying their trade." The apartment was the only accommodation the family could afford. Thousands of people were unemployed, many of them homeless. They begged in the streets. Prostitution was a big problem in many of the major cities during the war, and would be for some time after. Many other people did whatever they could to survive during the war years.

Oskar wound up in the hospital less than a year after moving to Toronto. The stress from the loss of his inheritance and the family's farm, his imprisonment, and the death of his youngest had been mounting up for years. He had over three-quarters of his stomach removed at St. Joseph's Hospital because it was so badly ulcerated.

My aunt told me that Oskar's temperament had also changed considerably. He would sit in the kitchen listening to the news of the war on radio while the family ate. He was always hopeful that good news would come, and his inheritance would be there at the end of the war. He would yell at Bernard and Bernice, telling them to "shut up," and then he would run to the sink and throw up.

Early in 1944, well before D-Day and the campaign to liberate western Europe, oversupply of cordite, guncotton and TNT for the Canadian and British armed forces caused production at Nobel to be halted. Many of the employees that were laid off, now hooked on regular pay cheques and the comfortable work environment that went with war work, moved to distant points to take other jobs. Some were hired by A.V. Roe, the builder of the Lancaster at Malton, and others went to Chalk River where jobs were available. Laid off DIL workers who chose or were forced to hang around Parry Sound were rewarded in mid-1944 when there was a callback of employees to produce cordite for the United States armed forces.

During the evening of August 14, 1945—on V-J Night—the celebration of the defeat of Japan, a grain elevator at Depot Harbour somehow caught fire. The blaze spread to sheds filled with the now unneeded Nobel cordite. An estimated 56 train carloads (close to 4 million pounds) of cordite exploded. Luckily, there were people on the scene that were familiar with cordite's behaviour. They opened doors and downsized a potential explosion of atomic bomb proportions into a mere holocaust. That night, the DIL treated the people of Parry Sound and area to one of the greatest fireworks displays ever. It turned the night sky into daylight, and one report said that it was seen as far as 24 miles away. Rumours persisted for many years that orders had come down "to dispose of the excess cordite by whatever means necessary." [a013]

5.
CANADA AFTER WORLD WAR II

The war was over in 1945. In the six years of war, Canada had enlisted over 730,000 men and women. Of those, more than 45,000 gave their lives for the cause of peace and freedom. Many other soldiers returned home from the war broken in mind and spirit. For each man killed in battle, almost four others had been wounded.

It took everything the Allies had to stop Nazi Germany. From 1939 to the end of the war, the Allies dropped 3.4 million tons of bombs on Germany, mostly in industrial cities. We also know that there were many large German civilian cities that were bombed.

Worldwide casualty estimates vary widely from several sources. Military deaths were 15 million soldiers, with over 25 million wounded. There were an additional 45 million innocent people that died as well. In China alone, there may have been as many as 50 million deaths. These people had no choice or say in the matter.

"Is this the legacy of war?" is something I have asked myself many times over the years.

Austria had not been an active participant in World War II. It was invaded by Nazi Germany. The mountains had shielded much of Austria from Allied bombing. All of Oskar and Theresia Bendl's brothers and sisters in Austria survived the war.

Soldiers returned to Canada to an uncertain future. Many found that their relationships or marriages were gone. Most Canadians had reason to celebrate, however. The war was over.

Oskar also developed trouble with his breathing. It may have been caused by the smoke of the burning of bandages or working with sulphuric acid at the CIL plant many years before. He got a job at the Canadian Standards Association (CSA), but was let go shortly later "because of his age."

Canada's economy after the Second World War differed considerably from that of the First World War. The government had prepared for the return of its soldiers much better. The economy was sluggish getting started, however.

Oskar took a job as a night watchman minding sheep on one of the Toronto islands. It was the only one he could find. Less than a year later, Oskar got a job as a janitor at Dodd's Kidney Pills in Toronto. The owner got to know Oskar and helped him secure a better paying job as a janitor in a small professional building in downtown Toronto.

In the late 1940s, Theresia got a job as a cleaning lady in a movie theatre, sweeping up popcorn and candy wrappers after the children's movie matinees. I remember her giving my sister, Judith, and I little trinkets that she had swept up from the theatre floor in the 50s. There were marbles, a sheriff's badge, and other little things. I was old enough to know that our grandparents were poor. I was six or seven years old at the time. I thought it was awfully sweet that she had thought of us and had saved something for me. Most of you, my cousins, had not even been born. This is the type of woman your grandmother was.

Oskar and Theresia on Richmond Street, Toronto, 1950

So what really happened to Oskar's inheritance from his mother?

Oskar wrote to the government of Canada asking for compensation, since it was they that had prevented him from going to Czechoslovakia to collect his inheritance in the first place. Canada had not even gone to war with Germany until six months after his mother's death. The government had also taken his land. Oskar got nowhere with the Canadian government. They told Oskar to try and seek compensation from the communist Czech government. Oskar wrote the lawyer that had handled his mother's estate and heard nothing.

One day while he was at work at the professional building, one of the workers that was leaving the building befriended him. The worker got to know Oskar in the following weeks. He could not believe what had happened to Oskar and his family. That person called *The Globe and Mail* newspaper. A reporter visited the Bendl's apartment and took the story. I still have that newspaper clipping in my files. The article will explain to you what really happened to his inheritance.

The article was called "Wait A Minute! IT MIGHT HAVE BEEN"

The reporter wrote: "Oskar Bendl is a janitor in a downtown Toronto building. To the tenants of the building, the sturdy, grizzle-headed little man with the stubborn German accent probably appears as

FIVE ROWS OF BARBED WIRE

a grey shadow, a menial figure who was marked from birth for his humble job.

But there was a day when Oskar Bendl looked forward to inheriting a comfortable fortune.

6-million crowns! He became a Canadian citizen on August 24, 1934." The article went on...

[The following are in Oskar's words, as they were given to the reporter that day.]

Oskar fingered the ragged fringe of the cuffs of his shirt. He told the reporter, "My mother had many jewels and much real estate. Though there were eight children in the family, we each had a considerable amount of money under my mother's will." Again, he fingered the ragged cuffs of his shirt. "I applied to Ottawa for permission to go to Czechoslovakia. But it takes a big government a long time to take action on small matters, and before permission came through, Canada was at war with Germany." He went on to say, "and because I am of German descent, I was sent to an internment camp for three years." A very uncertain smile toddled across Oskar's face. "I used to dream about my good fortune. I knew my sister, Sophie, had placed the many jewels and money that were to be mine in a bank vault in a little town called Schlackenworth in Bohemia, and that she had the receipt. I decided I would take a portion of their value of the real estate. A few thousand dollars would have been enough to give me and wife and my five children a new start."

"But after the war, the world was mixed up, and messy like a spilled stew." That summer, Oskar's lawyers received a letter with permission from the Department of External Affairs to attempt to get his property from the communist country of Czechoslovakia.

Oskar had written to Dr. Krizek, the lawyer that had handled his mother's estate. Oskar received a letter in reply written by a Dr. Karel Rudik, a Czech lawyer in Carlsbad. The letter read: "I have been appointed substitute for Dr. Krizek who has not been admitted to the newly-formed Provincial Chamber of Barristers and Solicitors in Prague. It is my duty to protect the interests of Dr. Krizek's clients until they appoint another attorney." Oskar stopped reading for a moment. "Dr. Krizek is probably not a [communist] party member," he said. "That's what that means".

Oskar resumed reading. Dr. Rudik wrote: "I want to inform you how this case stands at present. It appears you have not been informed yet, that the administration and probate re: your mother, Anna deceased, had not been brought to an end by the end of World War II. As your mother was of German origin, the whole of the property was to be confiscated for the benefit of the Czechoslovak state. In such cases, no distribution of property to heirs and legatees takes place. Under these circumstances, I am afraid I cannot advise you to deal with this affair any longer. In general, I hold this case to be closed." Oskar stopped reading. "The friends of the working man have swiped the money, as you might say," he said.

> [Author's note: After the First World War, the German-dominated Austria-Hungary was dismembered, and Sudeten Germans found themselves living in the new country of Czechoslovakia (first republic 1918–1938). When Czechoslovakia was reconstituted after the Second World War, the Sudeten Germans were largely expelled (1938–1939). Oskar's inheritance was in a bank as war broke out in 1939. Anna Bendl was of German descent, and the Czech state seized the money of the Sudeten Germans at the end of the war.]

Oskar then read the last paragraph from Dr. Rudik's letter: "I shall send you Dr. Krizek's and my account as soon as possible." Oskar smiled a little, lowered the letter and said, "It is a very small satisfaction," he said, "but I have no intention of paying the account." [a014]

All of the members of the Bendl family pitched in to make life livable for the family. My mother, Joyce, got a job at the Bell Telephone Company as an operator in Toronto. Shortly later, she married my father in 1948.

I remembered that in 1949 my father bought my mother a 1949 Rogers Majestic AM shortwave tube radio. She loved country music as a teenager growing up in Muskoka. My father ran an antenna wire outside and soldered the wire on the eavestrough of the house they rented so she could receive the broadcast music from Nashville, Tennessee.

In 1952, my parents moved to London, Ontario. In London, my father managed a photofinishing company for a Toronto company, and my mother was hired by the Bell Telephone Company in London as an operator. The first people that befriended our parents in London were of Ukrainian descent, the Kozaks and the Szabo Halos. They were hard-working people that had come to Canada and had originally worked out on the prairies. They were some of the many Ukrainians that had come to Canada in years preceding World War II. They had also been forced into labour on Canada's prairies.

In 1952, Oskar, Theresia, and the twins moved into an apartment above an appliance store at Maitland and Bloor Streets in Toronto. That area of Toronto in the early 1950s also was not a desirable area to live in. It was also an area frequented by prostitutes and "shady individuals." But, it was all the family could afford at that time.

Bernice married a butcher named Gord. Oskar and Theresia, and Gord and Bernice shared in the costs of the rent and food. Life was starting to improve, but it really wasn't easy for them.

Many companies that had increased production during the war, cut it at the end of the war, laying off people. Tens of thousands of Canadians were unemployed, and many of them were homeless. The major cities were plagued with beggars everywhere. I remember seeing this even as a young child. . The steel, aluminum, and chemical businesses were an example of this after the initial surge of business following the end of the war.

Thousands of the people that had been imprisoned during the war were also unemployed or worked in menial, low-paying jobs. Many of the formerly imprisoned men never worked again.

Government articles have stated that the returning soldiers and their families were eager to buy new cars, homes, and appliances. Actually, many them could not afford to buy a new car or home. It took many years for many people to replace their old car or take the "plunge" on a home. The housing boom did not take place until the 1950s.

In about 1954 or 1955, the economy began improving and the massive building of new homes began. The Canadian government made a conscious effort to avoid a repeat of the chaos that had come on the heels of the end of World War I. The government forced companies to hire veterans and provided low interest loans to them.

In the late 1950s, I wondered even then why growth seemed so slow. I had visited cities like Chicago, Philadelphia, and others, and saw that the economy there seemed much better. Naturally, years later, I learned that the United States had been the biggest benefactor of the war.

My mother and father could not afford a home until 1955, ten years after the war. My father made $90 a week, and that was considerably more than what many people were working for at the time. In the 1950s, $60 million worth of new housing was built, more than what had been built in the previous 25 years.

I noticed in the late 50s that Oskar had even started to laugh. It was my father, Jack Fréchette, that taught the Bendl's how to laugh again. They had been through so much over the years, they had even forgotten how to laugh.

The baby boom after the war necessitated the building of many schools in the 1950s.

Many of the buildings in Canada's cities were very old and I remember many restaurants still used oilcloth for tablecloths.

Many Europeans did not speak their native languages in public even after the war, particularly if they spoke German. If someone was caught speaking a language other than English or French, someone would shout out at them, "Speak English!" or they would say "Go back to your country!" They were still discriminated against even after the war. These people were often called "DPs," or Displaced Persons, by people of British descent. The immigrants would even be called that into the early 1960s, I recall. Today, I have friends that are Jewish and Muslim that tell me the problem still exists seventy-three years after World War Two.

FIVE ROWS OF BARBED WIRE

I remember visiting my grandparents and Gord and Bernice at the apartment on Maitland Street in Toronto in the 1950s. I learned at a young age that my grandparents possessed fine European values, something that doesn't seem to exist today. They were polite, and good listeners. Perhaps they were good listeners because they had suffered so much in their lives. Other people's happiness made them happy. Or, perhaps it hid the sorrow in their lives.

Theresia Bendl   *Oskar Bendl*

If my grandparents did talk about Ripples or the loss of Oskar's inheritance, it was only in hushed tones with the adult members of the family or close friends. As a child, I often listened to their conversations with my ear "glued to the door" in another room.

I never saw my grandfather as being bad tempered. He spoke with a heavy German accent, and he was, I believe, hard of hearing. When I visited them, as soon as we arrived, the rye bread, liverwurst, and Velveeta cheese was put on the table, and tea and coffee was made. My grandfather always called my grandmother "Mom." She made excellent apple strudel and wiener schnitzel, and she was always asked to make them when she visited other people's homes. After she knew where everything was kept, she could "whip them up in a flash."

My grandparents went for a walk one evening, and witnessed a cat being hit by a car. Oskar and Theresia did not know what to do. The cat was "out cold," but it was still breathing. Oskar picked the cat up and they took it back to their apartment. The cat could not walk and the Bendl's could not afford a veterinarian. Oskar said, "Give it some time." They fed the cat by hand and in about a week and half "Whitey" was standing on his own four feet. Whitey ate table scraps and whatever was left over. Theresia fed Whitey peas, potatoes, and whatever meat she could scrape off the bones. Occasionally, Whitey got a can of Puss & Boots when they could afford it. That is the type of people my grandparents were. And you know, Whitey the cat lived with them for over twenty-two years.

My grandfather never really talked to me much when I was a child. He would ask me how I was doing in school and I would say "OK." He would usually laugh and say "Ya." Years later I was able to have conversations with him, but they were usually interrupted by someone else that was visiting at the time.

Mr. Koenig, a fellow POW from Ripples, lived in Toronto and visited the Bendl's occasionally with his wife. I remember he was called "Dr. Koenig" in the late 1940s and 1950s. "Dr. Koenig" was not a real doctor. He was a quack, but he did help many of the families that could not afford medical help after the war. Dr. Koenig even performed some minor surgeries as well. I was told years later that he did them quite well.

My grandfather was sociable with family and guests, but invariably would "slip off to his room to paint" at some point. He never lost his passion for oil painting. He painted hundreds and hundreds of oil paintings in his lifetime. My father was a photo-finisher and gave him canvases that had been removed from photo print drying machines. Oskar cut the canvases and then stretched and nailed them on wood frames that he had made. He wasn't much of a carpenter, though. My father gave him a battery-operated slide viewer that Oskar used to view a slide with when he was painting.

I remember sleeping in my grandfather's room, and the smell of the oil paints. I remember him coming into the bedroom to paint. I was supposed to be asleep, but I watched him. He sat in the dark with only a side light, and began to paint. Often, he would slip a Fisherman's Friend lozenge into his mouth. I remember the strokes of his brush were long and slow, with a perfectly steady hand. Occasionally he dabbed at the canvas. I watched him paint for a long time before I fell asleep. I did not know the history of his painting skill because I was too young at that time.

Original Oil Painting by Oskar Bendl

Original Oil Painting by Oskar Bendl

Original Oil Painting by Oskar Bendl

Oskar Bendl never had his name in the "who's who of painting," The Royal Ontario Museum (ROM) because he could never afford to have his name published in the ROM.

Oskar sold small paintings in the local park. He was occasionally commissioned to paint larger scenes for people that had more money, though I don't believe he ever made a lot of money for his paintings.

Oskar was primarily a landscape painter. But he did paintings of people as well, including many of Jesus Christ and the crucifixion. I remember one painting of Jesus Christ that any Catholic church in the world would have loved to own. Oskar had the ability to change the very traits of his painting styles. I learned this over the years as my knowledge of the arts improved, and after viewing hundreds of his and other artists' paintings.

Today, I look at many oil paintings in galleries, shops, and boutiques for $300, $400, and $500, and I smile. It is a sad fact that Oskar never made a lot of money for his beautiful paintings in his lifetime, but today he would be a very rich man.

Today, Oskar's paintings hang in homes, and doctors' and lawyers' offices all over the world. Many of his paintings are here in Canada, in the United States, and in many countries in Europe. Recently, we even learned of one in Russia.

His paintings are signed "Oskar Bendl" or "O.B." There are a few that are signed "Oscar Bendl," though his name was Oskar. As well, there are many that were not signed, and it is not known why. The paintings that were not signed, however, are identifiable by myself and a couple other family members.

In the late 1950s, Gord and Bernice had managed to save enough money to put a down payment on a new home in Scarborough, Ontario. Oskar and Theresia lived with their daughter and her husband. In the early 1960s, Oskar painted in the basement of the home. He was commissioned several times to paint reclining nudes for men that had bars in their recreation rooms. In the 1940s and 50s there were bars that had those type of paintings, which faced the patrons in the bar. I was a young teenager and was not supposed to have seen those paintings at my young age, but I did!

FIVE ROWS OF BARBED WIRE

I remember those paintings as comparable to the very magic of the famous Austrian painter Ernst Klimt. I strongly believe that Oskar was influenced by Ernst Klimt and Alois Arnegger, another famous Austrian oil painter of his time. The traits of both of those very famous painters are evident in many of Oskar's paintings.

By the early 1960s, the baby boom was fading, and by 1967 it was over. In 1961, Canada's economy was on the upswing, though many Canadian cities still lagged behind American cities. Canada's per capita income was 40% behind that of the United States.

Lou became a steamfitter, and before long he was a foreman. In the 1960s, he had worked on every major project in Canada as a foreman. He had worked on the Welland Canal, the Athabasca Tar Sands, the Douglas Point Nuclear Project, and other projects.

Bernard wanted to become a forest ranger. My father told him that he should go to school and become a doctor. The Bendl's did not have enough money to put Bernard through university. He went out and got two jobs to pay for his own university education. Bernard even developed the energy and enjoyed going to the local park to teach baseball to the underprivileged neighbourhood boys. Bernard went through medical school after finishing university, and went on to specialize in dermatology.

In his career, Dr. Bernard Joseph Bendl discovered over 100 diseases, and wrote white papers on all of them. His papers are read to this day by dermatologists around the world. If you are savvy, you can Google uncle Bernard's history on the Internet. In the 1980s, he served as the personal physician to the Crown Prince of Saudi Arabia. He was there for almost four years, which was almost a year longer than any previously serving physician to the Crown Prince. He had done very well for a young man that once only had the dream of becoming a forest ranger. He would also always remember where he had come from until the day he died.

About 1961, Lou decided that he wanted to build a home for his parents beside his farm just outside of Campbellford, Ontario. Campbellford is in Northumberland County. It is beautiful countryside with many rolling hills. There was a hillside about 500 feet from his home with a pasture in between. It was a fitting place to build a home for a couple that had come from Austria. Behind where the house would sit, were rolling hills with a woodlot at the back.

The plans were drawn up for the home and the excavation for the foundation, which was in the side of the hill. Lou and the husbands of his sisters, including my father, worked on the construction of the bungalow every weekend the following year. Gord, Bernice's husband, and Ken, Margaret's husband, lived in Toronto. Jack, my father, of course lived in London, Ontario. So, it was a weekend project from spring until autumn.

I remember driving to Gord and Bernice's in Scarborough on Friday nights, picking up Gord and Ken, and driving to Campbellford to work on the home on the Saturdays and Sundays. The construction took all summer. Oskar was not skilled with power tools, so he was relegated to chores of holding boards or fetching things.

I did witness my grandfather pick up an axe one day and "eye" a tree. He always walked kind of hunched over. He always wore baggy grey wool pants, and a blue plaid flannel shirt it seemed. He looked around the area of the tree and began to swing that axe. It was a good-sized tree. I was shocked at the sight of this short, frail, elderly man swinging the axe, and how quickly he took that tree down. It was evident when the tree had come down, that it had landed exactly where he wanted it to. None of the other trees or even the scrub around it had been damaged where the tree fell.

The home was finished, and it was a beautiful, well-constructed bungalow that overlooked the pasture and the road. Oskar and Theresia had their own home again after so many years, and it was "a little bit of Austria." Oskar painted and often wandered in the hills surrounding their home. There were herbs and many berries in the hills, and of course Oskar knew which ones they could eat because the Bendl's had come from Austria.

Original Oil Painting by Oskar Bendl

Original Oil Painting by Oskar Bendl

Original Oil Painting by Oskar Bendl

In their senior years, Oskar and Theresia walked the two miles into Campbellford to do their grocery shopping. If they got tired, they would sometimes stop and sit on a bench a farmer had put out by the road. All of the Bendl family members had been good walkers from their years living in Nobel. The Bendl's had never owned a car.

Oskar rented a small, old storefront in downtown Campbellford to sell his paintings. He displayed them in the store window. But Campbellford was a small farming town community. Farmers in the area in the 1960s were not really keen on purchasing oil paintings. Oskar sold some paintings in his store, though I don't believe he made a lot of money. I suspect he spent much his of time just painting.

Problems with the home developed in the winter three years later. It had been built on a hillside that contained a lot of sand and gravel. When it rained, the water table grew and pressure on the foundation of the home increased. The foundation cracked in a couple places and water seeped into the basement. It was decided that the repairs should not be done then as the ground was beginning to freeze. Sadly, my grandparents had to move out of their home until the repairs could be done.

In 1965, Gord and Bernice built Oskar and Theresia an apartment in the basement of their home in Scarborough, and they moved back to Scarborough for the winter.

On Christmas Day 1965, Oskar and Theresia were having Christmas dinner with their grandchildren Gordie and Susie, Gord and Bernice. Part way through the dinner, Oskar stood up from the dinner table, gasped, and fell to the floor. An ambulance was called and Oskar was taken to Scarborough General Hospital. He had suffered a massive stroke.

Bernice called my mother, notifying her of what had happened. We were having Christmas dinner at the Kozak's in London. We drove to the hospital in Toronto immediately that night.

All of the Bendl children were there with their families, and later that night, Bernard flew in from Vancouver, British Columbia.

I saw my grandfather take his last breaths. He had had a massive stroke and it wasn't pretty. It was heart wrenching. None of the family could stay in the room for more than a few minutes. He had led a very sad, painful life. He never regained consciousness. Oskar Bendl died two days later, on December 27, 1965.

My mother took the death of her father particularly hard, she was the second oldest. She was old enough to remember her parents' harsh lives. As well, she knew that they had always been "as poor as church mice." My mother would remember that until the day she died.

Oskar was survived by his wife Theresia and their children Lou, Joyce, Margaret, Bernard, and Bernice, and several grandchildren.

Bernice and Gord had two children at the time, Susie and Gordie. In the years following, they adopted three more children, including a brother and sister. Oskar and Theresia had lived with Bernice for many years, and Theresia continued after Oskar's death. Bernice Bendl had never forgotten where she came from.

After Oskar died, my mother hired a German genealogist, a Dr. Ing. Hans Mariacher, in West Germany to trace the family tree. It took years. When she received the family tree, the whole family was shocked. Oskar had known his family tree all along. Lou told me in 1998, that Oskar had even known the battles his great-great grandfather, von Kamper, had fought Napoleon in.

In 1969 a silver tea set given to my parents as a wedding gift by Oskar and Theresia was stolen from my parents home. My mother took it very hard, as she had known how hard her parents had worked to buy the gift for them.

As a child and teenager, I remember my mother receiving huge tins of delicious cookies from her aunts in Germany and Austria every Christmas. The boxes were postmarked Österreich Bundespost. My mother had corresponded with her aunts in the old country for decades with the help of a neighbour, Audrey Koeglar, who spoke and read German.

Theresia Bendl had a stroke and passed away on February 1, 1974. We had given her all the love we could in her last years, though you wish at times that you had given more. Our grandparents' lives had been a journey to living hell on earth. They gave us their love—it was all they could give us—and we loved them dearly. They were sweet people and did not deserve the hell that their journey to Canada had brought to them.

In the late 1970s, my mother could afford to fly to Germany to visit her aunts and uncles that she had never met. All but two lived in Germany by that time. Two of her uncles had remained in Carlsbad, then controlled by Czechoslovakia. The husband of one of my mother's cousins drove my mother to Carlsbad to visit them. They even visited the Bendl China factory, which had been turned into a museum. The museum had many samples of the fine china that had been made there. While at the museum, the history of the china factory was explained to her. Of course, she already knew the history of the factory. She knew it had been seized from the Bendl family decades earlier by the communist government.

My mother had forgotten all of her German. She had not spoken it for over 44 years. Over the next two years, she learned how to read, write, and speak German all over again. She began flying to Munich every year to visit her aunts and uncles. She particularly loved going to Wetzlar to shop. One of her aunts even offered to sign over her house to my mother if she would bring my father to Germany. This is the type of people Oskar's sisters were. When our mother visited her aunts, the aunt's neighbour's children always came to their door wanting to meet the lady from Canada. She loved visiting her aunts and she visited them all until they had all passed away.

*Shlackenwerth Church Postcard
Painted by Oskar Bendl 1924*

Schlackenworth Church, 2017 from Google Maps

With the fall of the Soviet Union in 1989, Lou Bendl received a letter from the Czech government asking him if he was interested in purchasing the Bendl China factory in Carlsbad, Czechoslovakia. Naturally, Lou had no interest in the purchase of a business in a former communist country. He forwarded the letter to Bernard, who also had no interest in such a purchase. In 1989, Ludwig Bendl's china factory had been in business for 210 years and had survived two World Wars!

In the 1980s, my mother and father purchased a large cottage property on Little Whitefish Lake, just south of Parry Sound. Little Whitefish Lake is situated between Lake Joseph and Lake Rousseau. There are many cottages owned by Hollywood actors in this area of Muskoka. Raquel Welch, Kurt Russell and Goldie Hawn are a few of the actors that owned cottages on Lake Joseph. The cottage our parents owned was a beautiful chalet with 300 feet of frontage on the lake. The lake's water was pristine clear. It too was "a little bit of Austria." It had all been a surprise for my mother. They drove to Parry Sound and had a coffee with a man in a restaurant who turned out to be a real estate agent. My father had planned that afternoon out very well!

My father always was a "confront your fears" type of individual. "There is nothing to fear," he always said. I believe he wanted my mother to have good memories of her childhood in Nobel, and he confronted her with it. He did the very same with me as a shy, young, travelling salesman. I was still shy, but I stood before the very people that could turn me away, and hid my shyness. In spite of that shyness, I was always a member of the President's Club for the companies that I worked for. It was my father that made me believe that nothing was insurmountable. He did the same for my mother that day. They purchased the cottage. Less than a year later, my mother had learned to love the area that had been a living nightmare in her childhood.

I remember walking down the main street of Parry Sound with my father one sunny summer afternoon. As we walked along, an attractive older woman in a summer dress and straw hat walked towards us. My father nudged me and whispered, "Ursula Andress." As the woman passed, she turned, smiled, and said hello to me. It actually was Ursula Andress! I almost tripped on the sidewalk.

Muskoka is beautiful in the summer and autumn, and we enjoyed many weekends there. My parents drove into Parry Sound several times a week, and even Nobel during the summer months. They dined out in Parry Sound often. Twice they even met and talked to women that had gone to school with my mother over 50 years earlier. The women did not know of all the horrors the Bendl's had lived through, and she did not tell them. The restaurant visit was a good time for my mother and the other women as well. They talked for hours.

My mother's sister, Margaret Bendl died of cancer on September 29, 1990. She and her husband, Ken, had always been good to all of their nieces and nephews. I remember fishing with Ken on May long weekends since my childhood, and his tremendous patience. Since I was a child, Ken had acted as a Santa at Christmas time in department stores in Toronto. Margaret and Ken both had also never forgotten where they came from.

In 1996, while visiting my parents' cottage, I decided that I wanted to drive to Nobel and see my grandparents' former property for myself. I told my mother that I was "going for a drive." I did not tell her where I was going, as I had always known that the name "Nobel" triggered something in her. I remember when I was young watching my mother washing dishes and singing while she did it. She loved country music, and would softly sing. She had a beautiful voice. Sometimes the singing would kind of slow down, or stop, and you could tell her thoughts had drifted to sad ones; you could see it in her eyes. My mother Joyce was always considered very "ladylike," but did you know that she could whistle loud, like a guy, when I was young? It always made me laugh because I could never whistle.

In 1966, after Oskar's death, the government had no further use for the Bendl property and returned it to Lou. The property had been taken from his father Oskar over 25 years earlier. The government and Orenda had used it for twenty years. The government of Canada kept it for another six years before returning it to the rightful owners. No compensation was offered for the buildings that they had burned, the contents of the home, the livestock, or even the money they had looted from Bendl's bank account. Naturally, the whole family had many bad memories of what had taken place in 1940. Lou sold the property a few years later, as it did not have any potential as farmland, or anything else for that matter.

The former Bendl property is just south of Nobel on the outskirts of town. It is on the east side of the highway. The Orenda buildings are still visible from the highway. Today, it and the other surrounding property is privately owned.

The Former Bendl Property 1926–1940 in 1997

There were many "No Trespassing" signs on the fence of the property. I am a curious individual and it got the better of me. Nothing was going to stop me from seeing the land that my grandparents had once owned. The trouble was though, I was confronted with a 10-foot-high fence with barbed wire on the top. I found a piece of canvas in my car and walked along the ditch looking for a spot where I could slide myself under the fence. Once in, I reached back under the fence to retrieve my camera.

I had heard lore of non-detonated ordinance on the property. I found a trail and followed it, seeing a pop can here, a beer bottle there. I felt relatively safe because I knew that the property had been visited before. I took about 30 photos and have included a couple of them in this book. This includes one I took inside the building where the Avro Arrow's Iroquois jet engine was tested. Orenda tested its engines here until early 1959. The Avro Arrow CF-105 was the most advanced jet interceptor in the world at the time. It was entirely designed and built in Canada and was the fastest jet in the world at that time. The Avro Arrow project was cancelled by Prime Minister John Diefenbaker on February 20, 1959. The cancellation of the project threw 50,000 Canadians out of work and destroyed what could have been a prosperous technical future for Canada.

Inside the Orenda Iroquois Jet Engine Test Building

I wandered around the large property for several hours. I don't believe that much of the Bendl property was actually used by the government, but perhaps the explosives plant had tested some ordinance in places. By chance I even stumbled across the remains of where the Bendl home had stood over fifty years earlier. I paused, my mind seemed blank. Then, thoughts of my grandmother and the horror she must have felt the day when the home was set ablaze, swept over me. It was a strange experience. Moments later, my mind went blank again and all I heard were the birds chirping. There were pieces of rotting, burned wood here and there. I resisted the thought of even considering anything as a souvenir. Basically, there was nothing there but bad memories. Nature had taken over this area many decades earlier. It was sad, but I felt satisfied that our grandparents and our mothers or fathers had lived there many years before; I left the property. This had been Bendl land from 1926 to 1940.

In the 1980s and 90s, we owned a camera shop and photo lab in Hanover, Ontario. Of course, my mother and father visited us often. After both "popping" into the store to say hello, my mother was off to "visit the town's shops." They enjoyed giving the small-town merchants their business. My mother found several merchants that spoke German. When they found out she was Austrian and spoke German, they remembered her by name when she visited again.

While living in Hanover, a customer that was an executive at a nearby German company translated our family tree from German to English for us. He had studied the Napoleonic battles at the University of Vienna, and of course, he too recognized, and knew of von Kamper's history. This gentleman's name is at the top of family tree that I provided in The Bendl History.

While living in Hanover, I had an older customer that visited our shop often to have photo prints copied. He had been a German soldier during WWII, and had carried a camera and taken many photos. My staff and I always enjoyed his frequent visits to our shop. He was very friendly and outgoing, and often looked at the photos in the store, and shared his photos and stories with us. He had taken photos at different places including the Tea House and the Crow's nest. I knew that the photos we had copied at our store were originals; they were too good to be copies, and he was in many of the photos.   [name withheld]

On another occasion, I had a tall, elderly customer from a neighbouring village come to my shop to have photos copied. A few days later he returned to pick up his order. He opened the package to look at the copies we had made and showed me a couple. I looked at the photos again and looked up at the man. He smiled. I knew then that he was a former SS officer during the war. I was speechless for a few seconds. He returned to our shop often to have copies made. The man always opened his orders to look at in the store, and we had many interesting discussions about his photos. On one of his visits, I came right out and asked if he had ever shot a civilian. He told me no, but that he had once shot a German soldier. On another occasion, he had given an order for a soldier to be shot. Naturally, I took much of what he said with a "grain of salt." It was interesting for me to see the war "from the other side" briefly, though some of his stories and experiences of the war contrasted considerably from what we have learned here. The man would most probably be deceased by now, but I withhold his name.   [name withheld]

The ethics of my career have always prevented me from discussing customer's property or their names with others. I have mentioned this because it is significant, considering if the government of Canada had really checked the backgrounds of many immigrants after the war. My philosophy has always been that the war ended over 73 years ago. I believe in live and let live. But I do not consider the imprisonment of tens of thousands of naturalized Canadians as just another government mistake. I see it as cruel upper handedness, and that it was remarkably foolhardy.

We lived in Hanover for almost 17 years. My thirty-six-year career in photofinishing ended there in 1999 with advent of the digital age.

In March of 1998, my mother and father took a holiday to Puerto Vallarta, Mexico. One evening after dining out, they strolled on the sidewalk outside the shops. My mother noticed a poor looking soul with hunched shoulders walking on the other side of the street. Perhaps the man reminded her of her father. She said that she had to talk to him. She crossed the street and began talking to the man. The two of them walked a considerable distance. My mother had the man laughing. She pointed at my father, who was walking along the other side of the street. The man looked over, smiled, and nodded at him. She reached into her purse, pulled out a wad of pesos, and put them in the man's hand. The man shook his head, trying to get her to take the pesos back. My mother refused, forcing the pesos back into his hand. The two walked and laughed for quite a time. My father did not know what she had told the man, or even how much money she had actually given him. She said later that the man had told her that he had been poor all his life but was too ashamed to beg. Perhaps she told that man that her family had been "as poor as church mice," that her family were too ashamed to beg, and that one day everything in their lives changed. That is the type of woman our mother was. She always remembered where she had come from.

Three days later, after returning from that holiday in sunny Mexico, my mother had a stroke and died three days later, on March 9, 1998 in London, Ontario. My mother died precisely fifty-nine years to the day of her grandmother Anna's death.

Dr. Bernard Joseph Bendl died January 28, 2005 in Richmond, British Columbia. I recently learned from Bernice that, up until his death, Bernard had donated money yearly to the parks for underprivileged kids in Vancouver. He also had never forgotten where he had come from.

Lou Bendl died on January 4, 2014, in Campbellford, Ontario. Lou had a heart of gold throughout his life. He helped everyone he knew, dividing his time, and often not getting his own work done. He had even become philosophical about not getting many things done in his later years. He helped and guided his mother, brothers, and sisters through the war years while his father was imprisoned. Years later he built a home for his mother and father, so they would have something of their own. I will always remember the fishing trips I took in childhood to his island in the Kawartha Lakes. Throughout his life Lou possessed incredible patience for his family and other people. Lou had never forgotten where he came from and he will never be forgotten by family or anyone that knew him.

Today, the last of Oskar and Theresia's children, Bernice, is still living as I complete this book.

THE NEW BRUNSWICK INTERNMENT CAMP MUSEUM

In July of 2017, I drove to Fredericton, New Brunswick, to visit the site of the former Camp B70 (Ripples), and the New Brunswick Internment Camp Museum in Minto.

The former prison sight is on a country road about 34 km from Fredericton and 8 km from Minto. The road is paved, but not in very good condition. I am sure there are more homes there today than in 1940, but the area is pretty much as it was in 1940. It is heavily forested with many small swamps. It is rough country, much like it was seventy-seven years ago.

At the site of the former Camp B70, there is an old blue billboard stating that the site is the site of a former "internment camp." However, because it faces the road, it is not clearly visible from either direction and a person could drive by without even noticing it.

All that remains at the site of the former Prisoner of War camp is the concrete base of the prison's water tower. It is a large structure, as it supported thousands of gallons of water for the prisoners and the guards. Nature had taken this area over many years ago. All of the buildings on the site were either destroyed or sold and moved.

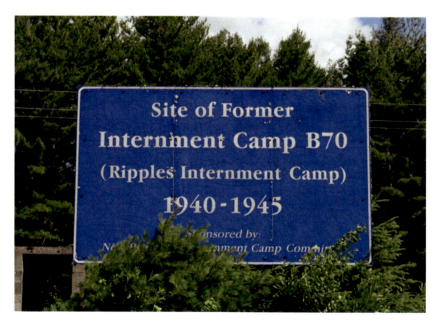

The site of the former Camp B70 Ripples, 1940–1945

All that remains is the former water tower and hiking trails.

The museum has turned it into a walking trail with many signs designating where the camp's various facilities were. I walked onto the trail a couple of hundred feet and felt satisfied that I had perhaps stood somewhere where my grandfather had stood 74 years earlier. I stood in a small clearing surrounded by pine trees and scrub. I was swarmed by mosquitoes, black flies, and deer flies, and ran back to the parking lot. There are also signs in the parking lot designating where everything had been in the camp during the war.

I was disappointed that the government of Canada has not designated the site properly, as a historical place. But that would be admitting to a mistake and—as we all know—the government doesn't like scrutiny for its mistakes. If you should visit this historical place,

I strongly advise the use of a good insect repellent. The deer flies, mosquitoes, and black flies are very friendly.

I drove 8 km further down that same road to the village of Minto, the location of the New Brunswick Internment Camp Museum. Minto was the location of one of Canada's coal mines between 1908 and 1984. Many miners lost their lives in this coal mine during the years it was in operation.

At the time of writing, the museum is located in the basement of the township office building. As you drive into the village, it is across from a Tim Horton.

When I arrived at the museum it was closed, but I was greeted by a museum guide in the parking lot. I was promptly invited into the museum when I told her I was a grandson of Oskar Bendl. Shortly later, I met the director-curator of the museum, Mr. Ed Caissie, who gave me a personal tour and explained various aspects of the museum and its artifacts.

After the war, the government dismantled the camp. They also destroyed whatever tools or utensils that were used in the camp fearing that people would take them and damage the local economy. The sight was bulldozed.

During the war and after, the camp had been mysterious to the people living around it; it lurked in their minds. All that remained was the huge concrete base of its water tower. In 1975, Mr. Caissie's curiosity got the better of him. He was a school teacher from Minto Junior High at the time. He organized an amateur archaeological dig on the site for students that were considered to be possible future dropouts. In the early 1990s, the federal government gave the school board money to establish a program for at-risk students. The money was to help develop self-esteem, pride in their work, and problem-solving skills. The following year, Mr. Caissie read the two-volume history of the camp by Ted Jones, called *Both Sides of the Wire*. Mr. Jones is also a school teacher from Fredericton. Mr. Caissie was further inspired by Mr. Jones' books. In the spring of 1994, students did more research of the camp and a scale model of the former camp was built giving all involved a better idea of where everything had been. Today, that model of the camp is a popular exhibit in the museum and exhibits throughout the province.

The project began in 1990. In the beginning, twenty of Mr. Caissie's students took part in the project, and later many other students wanted to get involved as well. The project was successful. The integration of the at-risk students with the rest of the student body became an amalgamation. The project was not just Mr. Caissie's project any longer; it had become everyone's project. Some sixty students had taken part in it. The school board has successfully used Mr. Caissie's approach in other schools in the district since that time.

The entire camp site was excavated to a depth of one metre, producing many artifacts that had been buried for decades. Many of the artifacts have axe marks on them, as the government had ordered the guards to destroy everything. They hastily tried to bury the history of the camp, it appears.

FIVE ROWS OF BARBED WIRE

Miniature vanity donated by my mother to the museum in 1997.

A model ship made by a Prisoner of War.

At the time of writing, the New Brunswick Internment Camp Museum has a floor space of 2,000 square feet and has over 600 artifacts in it today. The museum grows each year as more artifacts are found in garage sales, and many other artifacts are donated by local people or families of the former Prisoners of War. I believe the museum is now beginning to run out of space.

The museum floor space is relatively small, but there are a many of artifacts and pieces of art in the museum. The craftsmanship of the many European Canadian Prisoners of War is astonishing. There are model ships built inside liquor bottles, model boats with working motors, oil paintings, as well as utensils and tools used by the prisoners. The largest wall space dedicated to a prisoner's art is for our grandfather, Oskar Bendl, and the art section of the museum is dedicated in his name.

While visiting the museum, I personally donated four Oskar Bendl oil paintings to the them so that visitors may enjoy the beauty of his art.

Mr. Caissie has won several awards while on this project, including the National Award for Excellence in History. He has now worked on this project for over 40 years. He describes the camp as one aspect of a period in Canada's history that was "ugly, insane, and deadly." He hopes that people will consider well, and with open minds, stories associated to the camp that might be unsettling or spark defensive responses.

FIVE ROWS OF BARBED WIRE

In the museum, a mannequin wearing one of the prisoner uniforms.

A section of the camp layout floor display showing five rows of barbed wire.

Erica Leppmann, who teaches art at Oberland College in Ohio, spoke at the opening ceremonies of the museum in 1997. She had been researching the experiences of the prisoners of such camps throughout North America and noted the documentation of the camp at Minto as the best she has come across anywhere on the continent. [a015]

I feel that because of the significance of the museum and the very size of it, that it should have been in the provincial capital. However, one has to remember that the original camp site is just 8 km away and Mr. Caissie is "giving back" to the area he grew up in, that he taught in, and that he has given so much to. Mr. Caissie, with the help of many others, has preserved this sad but historical part of Canadian history.

When I left New Brunswick, I wanted to follow the footsteps that my grandfather had taken walking home from Ripples. I was driving on a modern highway that cuts through the near mountainous areas of western New Brunswick and eastern Québec. The distance today is 1,056 miles. It is a long trip by automobile. As I drove up the side of one of the mountains that day, I thought of Oskar walking home seventy-four years ago. I thought to myself that Oskar Bendl truly was an extraordinary man. His walk home was, a very long walk home.

BENDL FAMILY BIRTH & DEATH DATES

	BORN	DIED
Oskar Bendl	Jun 18, 1892	Dec 27, 1965
Theresia Bendl	May 21, 1903	Feb 1, 1974

....

Oskar and Theresia Bendl's Children

Lou Bendl	Feb 14, 1925	Jan 4, 2014
Joyce Bendl	May 5, 1928	Mar 9, 1998
Margaret Bendl	May 17, 1931	Sep 29, 1990
Bernard Bendl (twin)	Nov 26, 1936	Jan 19, 2005
Bernice Bendl (twin)	Nov 26, 1936	still living
Billy Bendl	1939	1943

6.
OSKAR AND THERESIA BENDL'S LEGACY

Oskar and Theresia Bendl have left our families with a beautiful legacy. Had they not made that hasty journey to Canada from Austria in 1925, over ninety-three years ago, we would not even be here today.

We, our children, and our grandchildren are Oskar and Theresia's legacy.

Though many of you had not been born in your grandfather's time or were very young when your grandmother was still living, I can assure you that they were delighted with each grandchild that was born. And I am sure they would further be delighted with the ones that had not yet been born. I know this because Linda and I remember the love they gave to us, the ones that had been born. I remember that Theresia was tickled pink by the birth of each and every one of you. I know this, because I remember the happiness in her eyes.

Though all of our mothers or fathers were poor when they were growing up, they were all brought up properly. As well, all of our mothers or fathers lived proper lives. Each and every one of Oskar and Theresia's children, our mothers or fathers, gave something back to the world. All of the Bendl's had never forgotten where they had come from.

Our grandfather's beautiful oil paintings are a legacy that lives on in our homes, and hopefully will live on in your children's and their children's homes. Today, Oskar's oil paintings are all over the world. They're in Canada, the United States, many countries of Europe, and in Russia. Many of Oskar's paintings are in the homes and offices of doctors and lawyers, and they also appear in the New Brunswick Internment Camp Museum in Minto, New Brunswick.

In our grandfather's honour, one thing that no one can ever dispute or take away from us is that we are descendants of Oskar and Theresia, as well as von Kamper. We are of Royal Austrian descent. It is all in our family tree.

The Bendl ancestry has been recorded and dates back to 1656, more than 362 years. Our grandparents' legacy lives on in us and our children. As of this writing, Oskar and Theresia Bendl are survived by their daughter, Bernice, seventeen grandchildren, thirty great-grandchildren, and dozens of great-great grandchildren.

7. SUMMARY

Oskar and Theresia Bendl, like tens of thousands of other immigrants, came to Canada in peace. They believed that Canada was a friendly country. Like immigrants that had come before them, they wanted a better life. Most had come to Canada to escape the never-ending wars in Europe. They were looking forward to a peaceful life, as I have shown you in this book.

The end of World War Two did not end the suffering or hardship for the tens of thousands that had been imprisoned, or their families. Nor did it end the bitterness for many of the POWs and their families. After the war, many were homeless, and thousands were unemployed for decades in a country that discriminated against many of their nationalities

Oskar and Theresia Bendl were poor from their journey to Canada in 1925 until their deaths, but we loved them dearly.

I have often wondered about the government's thinking during the war years. They had invited these nationalities to come here to live, offering them "free land," and years later their thinking became shallow, foggy, and distorted.

Considering 38,000 of its own citizens as "enemies or suspected terrorists" is not rational thinking. It is irrational thinking. I am sure most people would agree with that. The only conclusion one can come to is that the government developed a hatred of foreigners—its own citizens—their paranoia grew, and the sickness overwhelmed them.

Our grandparents and thousands of others had lived through the hell and starvation of World War I in Europe. Their journey to Canada brought them to the very doorstep of hell. The journey to Canada, for many, truly was a journey to living hell on earth. Tens of thousands of other European and Japanese Canadians suffered, and were also made poor by the actions taken against them by the government of Canada between 1939 and 1947. Many thousands of others lives were destroyed forever as well.

Uncle Lou told me that he felt that his father never held any contempt for being imprisoned during the war. I have my own beliefs about that, but I will leave that for you to think about and decide.

Though I cannot speak for my grandfather, I believe our grandfather Oskar remained a proud Austrian until the day he died.

A couple months ago, I visited a restaurant that had opened last summer. I was waited on by the owner, an older gentleman, and we had a brief, pleasant conversation. Though he spoke perfect English I knew he was an immigrant. The food and service was excellent in the restaurant, and I have visited it often since. The owner, Hamid, always greets me with a smile and talks to me. I asked Hamid about his life and how he wound up in Canada. He told me that he was born in Kabul, Afghanistan, and that his roots are Turkish-Mongolian, (Hazara). While living in Afghanistan he was a studying as medical student at Kabul University.

The Russians invaded his country, killing many people. He was jailed by the regime and was released after four years. When Hamid got out of prison, he wanted to leave the country. The Russians would not let him leave Afghanistan until he served almost five more years teaching army martial arts.

Hamid immigrated to Canada in 1992, and worked in the food service industry, and at small restaurants for low wages for many years. The food service industry is hard work, I know, as I have owned a restaurant. Today, Hamid owns his own restaurant, and he has transformed his restaurant, Mylo's. I have met his wife and his son, Milad, who also works shifts occasionally to help out. Hamid has other staff as well.

Hamid and his family have taken no one's jobs, but have created jobs for others.

Hamid and his family came from a war-torn country, just like the other immigrants of many years ago. They worked very hard to make something for themselves, just like the many other immigrants to Canada of many years ago. Hamid's philosophy, I believe, is very much like my own. We really don't care about race or colour. At the end of the day, we both agree what matters, is what good you did today. Who did you help?

We must always remember that everyone's family were immigrants to Canada at some point in time, including our own.

It is also important for us to always remember that very dark chapter in Canada's past because it was so cruel and so very wrong. But as the hands of the clock move forward for all of us, we're all aware that you cannot turn back the clock and reverse the mistakes and injustices of the past. We can only go forward with the hope of never making those same mistakes again.

I wish that that I could bring Oskar and Theresia and the family back, and give them all a big hug and kiss, and tell them that I love them. I'd like to tell them that maybe I have felt a little of the pain that the family suffered. However, knowing what I know, that would not even be possible. There never was a "black mark" on the Bendl Family, as our grandfather had once stated, the "black mark" is actually on the government of Canada.

Oskar and Theresia Bendl and tens of thousands other immigrants were betrayed by the very country they had trusted, Canada and its government.

> To my cousins,
>
> You now know why your mothers or fathers never told you about their childhoods in Nobel, Ontario, Canada.
>
> It is my hope that you hand this history of our grandparents' lives down to your children at an appropriate age if you feel fitting, so that our grandparents will never be forgotten.
>
> your cousin, Jackie

Always in our hearts, never to be forgotten.

FOR OSKAR AND THERESIA BENDL & FAMILY

For the Record
Submitted March 9, 2018

Millions of children around the world were left fatherless after WWII. In Europe alone over a million children were orphaned by the bombing raids of both the Allies, and Nazi Germany.

Orphaned German Children WWII
Bundesarchiv Foto 1945   [a17]

Sehr geehrte Leserin, sehr geehrter Leser,

vielen Dank, dass Sie mein Buch gelesen haben. Ich selbest kann nicht Deutsch lesen, schreiben oder sprechen, aber eine Freundin von mir hat diese Zeilen für mich ins Deutsche

Ich bin kein Schriftsteller und auch kein Historiker. Mir war jedoch daran gelegen, die Geschichte der Immigration meiner Großeltern von Österreich nach Kanada im Jahr 1925 zu erzählen. Ich wollte wiedergeben, wie viel Leid die Familie während des Zweiten Weltkriegs in Kanada durch die kanadische Regierung ertragen musste- auch in dem Bewußtsein, dass viele von Ihnen ebenfalls sehr gelesen haben, haben.

Die Geschehnisse, über die Sie in diesem Buch gelesen haben, haben sich wirklich so zugetragen.

Für eventuelle Irrtümer, die mir möglicherweise in Bezug auf die Geschichte des Napoleonischen Kriegs und des Ersten Weltkriegs unterlaufen sind, möchte ich mich entschuldigen—ich weiss, dass viele Europäer über wesentlich umfangreichere Kenntnisse der entsprechenden historischen Ereignisse verfügen.   [Verfasser]

Vielen Dank

ABOUT THIS BOOK

This book actually began over forty-six years ago, when I talked to my grandmother and took notes. I still have those handwritten notes in my files. Over the years I collected notes from all the members of the Bendl family. Many of my mother's brothers and sisters did not tell their children about their childhoods in Nobel, Ontario. My own mother did not tell my sister and I anything about her childhood. All my mother told us was "We were as poor as church mice." As I got older, I learned more.

Oskar Bendl, my grandfather, told me about the Second World War when I was a teenager. I learned most of the details of the family from my Uncle Lou over the years, as he had seen the events of the family's life and knew the history. Bernice, our aunt (still living), provided me with even more details over the last six years, making me believe that I could possibly even write this book for you. All I did was compare and connect the dots from the different family members. Friends that read the earlier manuscript told me that it was an incredible story and that I had to get it published. It truly is a sad, incredible story.

It has been an emotionally draining experience writing about my grandparents' lives, but I wanted to do this as a matter of record, for family and others. I have crafted no lies here. What you have read is true, and was handed down to me by my own family. They were honourable people.

From my studies over the last several years, I know there were thousands of others who suffered. Our grandparents' story is just one story. There are many others that have never been told, though most of those people are now deceased. Sadly, their stories will never be told. Sadly, the dust of time will hide the stories from their own family members and other Canadians forever.

I have told you our family's story in this book.

In closing, I would like to ask you, the reader, one question:

How would you feel if this had been done to your family, or even to you?

FIVE ROWS OF BARBED WIRE

Five Rows of Barbed Wire has pretty much been written from my memory of world history, and my own family history. The documented dates, cities, and statistics of world history are available in hundreds of papers and books in libraries.

I have credited the authors and articles that I have used excerpts from in this book.

I have withheld certain names as a courtesy to certain people, and have honoured the wishes of others that asked that their names not be published.

OTHER BOOKS

Further in-depth reading on Canada's Prisoner of War Camps in WWII

Both Sides of the Wire by Ted Jones, volume one
ISBN 0-920483-21-6

Both Sides of the Wire by Ted Jones, volume two
ISBN 0-920483-25-9

POW Behind Canadian Barbed Wire by David J. Carter
ISBN 0-9684111-0-X

Further in-depth reading on Canada's Prisoners of War in WWI

Blood and Salt by Barbara Sapergia
ISBN 978-2-55050-513-9

Further in-depth reading on the Histories of Europe and Napoleon Bonaparte

Pageant of Europe by Raymond Stearns
Library of Congress Catalog Card Number
61-10710

The Napoleonic Guide (online) by Richard Moore

CREDITS AND ACKNOWLEDGEMENTS

[a01] Moore, Richard-*The Napoleonic Guide, Leipzig battlefield*
[a02] from Wikipedia
[a03] Sanders D.
[a04] from Canadian govt. Archives
[a05] J. Graham Royde-Smith, U.S. War Department
[a06] The Parry Sound Library, History of Nobel and Local History
[a07] Bank of Canada BOC, currency conversions
[a08] from Canadian govt. Archives Canadian, military personnel WW2
[a09] Mitham, Peter for *The Daily Gleaner*, interview with Mr. Kallmann
[a10] Stranger-Ross, Jordan UOV, Canadian immigration of Chinese and Japanese
[a11] Stranger-Ross, Jordan UOV, Takahashis home, Victoria B.C.

[a12] Mulroney, Brian PM, apology speech to Japanese Canadians, 1988
[a13] *Metroland News Media*, article
[a14] *The Globe and Mail*, article, Oskar Bendl Inheritance Loss
[a15] Mitham, Peter for *The Gleaner*, Erica Leppmann, Oberland College, Ohio
[a16] Ted Jones, photo, Prisoner of War card
[a17] Bundesarchiv Foto 1945

FURTHER ACKNOWLEDGEMENTS, AND THANK YOUS:

Library and Archives Canada
Ted Jones, author *Both Sides of The Wire*
Ed Caissie, director and curator, New Brunswick Internment Camp Museum
Oskar & Theresia Bendl
Lou (Louis) Patrick Bendl
Bernice Bendl
Joyce Fréchette (nee Bendl), my mother
Margaret Bendl
Jack Fréchette Sr.
Wolfgang Preussner
Hamid
Katharina

Very Big Thank You To:
Pierre and Evelyn [last names withheld]
for information provided in the book.
You Made It Happen

ABOUT THE AUTHOR

Jack Fréchette is a retired photo-finisher, and lives in London, Ontario, Canada. His hobbies include his grandchildren, photography, political science, worldwide military, the arts, and the environment.